EAT AND STAY SLIM
WITH
SOUPS AND SALADS

EAT AND STAY SLIM

WITH

SOUPS AND SALADS

By

Purobi Babbar

Over 100 Recipes — Vegetarian & Non-Vegetarian
from all over the world
(tasted and tried)

VAKILS FEFFER AND SIMONS LTD.
Hague Building, 9, Sprott Road,
Ballard Estate, Mumbai 400 001.

First Printing: 1998

By the same Author

Rotis and Naans of India with Accompaniments
Amantran (Hindi)
The Flavours of China
Say Cheese for Better Health

Price : Rs. 135/-

ISBN 81-87111-09-7

Published by Mrs. Jean Trindade for Vakils, Feffer and Simons Ltd.
Hague Building, 9, Sprott Road, Ballard Estate, Mumbai 400 001.

Printed by Arun K. Mehta at Vakil & Sons Ltd.,
Vakils House, Sprott Road, 18, Ballard Estate, Mumbai 400 001.

Designed by Vakils Art Department.

CONTENTS

ACKNOWLEDGEMENTS

My Special Thanks to:-

1. Ramada Hotel Palm Grove, Mumbai.

2. Mr. V. Pathian, General Manager,
   Ramada Hotel Palm Grove, Mumbai.

3. Mr. Rabington Anklaswaria, F & B Manager,
   Ramada Hotel Palm Grove, Mumbai.

4. Mr. Thomas, Ramada Hotel Palm Grove, Mumbai.

5. Ms. Eneide Saccani Buttucchi, La Spezia, Italy.

6. Ms. Edelweiss Saccani Bubbar, La Spezia, Italy.

7. Mrs. Venere Avanzi.

8. Mr. K. J. Joseph, Indore.

9. Ms. Gloria Scapagnini, Rome, Italy.

10. Mr. Sergio Scapagnini, Rome, Italy.

Food courtesy   :   Ramada Hotel Palm Grove

Photography   :   Rashid Bhatkar

SOUP MAKING

Home made soup is not only delicious — it is also often extremely economical. Soup making depends on (a) careful preparation of stock and (b) judicious blending of the different flavourings so that none predominates, except the original flavours. In this chapter, you will find not only popular and original authentic recipes from all over the world but also exotic collection of unusually rich nutritious soups.

When preparing vegetable soups use those vegetables that are in season. There are no hard and fast rules for how much soup one should allow. If you are serving the soup with a substantial main course, you generally allow 1/3 pint of clear soup and 1/4 pint of thick soup. However, soup is to be the most filling part of the meal. Please ensure you use an average Indian teacup equivalent to 150 ml. for measurements.

Cold soup recipes come from hot countries and are best served in hot weather.

SALAD MAKING

The most delightful sight on a dining table is a well made salad. Vegetables for salad may be either cooked or raw and the most used are — lettuce, mustard and cress, water cress, cucumber, radish, tomato, spring onions, cauliflower and celery. The cooked vegetables used are beetroot, frenchbeans, green peas and other types of beans and asparagus. Cooked fish, eggs, meat, fruits and nuts may also be used in salad making. For raw vegetable salad, it is very essential that all vegetables should be fresh; green leaves should be washed, drained and thoroughly dried. Care should be taken not to bruise leaves and for this reason, they should never be cut with a knife but torn with the finger tips. A wooden spoon or fork should always be used for mixing. Dressings should be used just before serving unless recipe demands otherwise.

Side Salad:.

Although most popular, a side salad is a simple, green salad of crisp lettuce leaves, cucumber, green pepper and cress, dressed with plain French dressing. It goes with almost any dish. Today there are numerous side salads. Some are more elaborate than others but one has to use ones own sense to balance it. Obviously, a rich dish needs a simple salad to accompany it. Side salads should be attractively presented.

Main Course Salad:

Remember to serve a more elaborate and substantial salad with a simple green side salad and crusty French bread with flavoured butter. A main course salad can be a complete meal in itself; with addition of meat, cheese, pasta, rice, vegetables, fruits etc. A main course salad can be made easily and quickly and it is an ideal way of using up left overs of any of the above dishes. Aspic, jellied and moulded salads makes an excellent dinner or lunch dish.

In order to make a good salad certain points should be remembered. A clever and artistic touch demonstrates imaginative flair and masterly strokes of originality:

1. The ingredients used for the salad should be fresh, and not discoloured.

2. The dressing is a very important part of the salad. The usual mistake is too much dressing, swamping the salad instead of making it appetizing. No surplus dressing should be seen in the bottom of the bowl. Dressing should be used for flavour only.

3. The garnish makes the salad look more attractive and appetizing. A skillful garnish is always appealing to the eye. There are a few garnishes for the salads given in the next page.

4. Always place vegetables used for garnishing in a bowl of fresh water.

SOUP GARNISHES

Rules:

1. Before using 'Einlauf' make sure the soup is boiling as the egg mixture should curdle into large flakes, the moment it is added. Once you add 'Einlauf' in the soup it should not go on boiling. Remove from heat, cover and allow the soup to clear again.

2. Garnishes for clear soup are sometimes cooked separately in salted water, but also cooked with the soups, like dumplings.

3. For dropping dumpling mixture into soup dip the spoon into boiling water first to shape dumplings. Use two wooden spoons dipped in flour.

'EINLAUF' (EGG GARNISH)

- 4 tbsps. plain flour.
- 1 egg.
- 1 tbsp. milk.
- pinch of nutmeg.
- pinch of salt.

- Mix together in a bowl flour, milk and egg, making sure the mixture is free from any lumps.
- Add salt and nutmeg.
- Hold a perforated ladle over the soup and pass the mixture through it. Pieces should fall directly into the boiling soup. The mixture should curdle at once into large flakes. Remove from heat, cover and leave it to clear.

ALMOND RICE

PREPARATION TIME : 10 MINUTES	COOKING TIME : 30 MINUTES

- 3 cups (450 ml.) milk.
- 2 tbsps. ground almonds.
- 75 gms. rice washed and drained well.
- 4 tbsps. sugar.
- 3 drops lemon essence.
- ½ tsp. almond essence.
- pinch of salt.
- 1 tsp. butter.

- Heat milk in a sauce pan, add almonds, essence and butter. Bring to the boil.
- Add rice, cook gently until done. Should be thick.
- Add sugar and salt. Mix well.
- Press hot rice into small well greased moulds, keep warm for a few minutes and unmould. Serve with fruit soups instead of dumplings.

CHEESE CRUSTS

PREPARATION TIME : 15 MINUTES	COOKING TIME : 20 MINUTES

- 4-5 thin slices of bread.
- 1 cup (150 ml.) milk.
- 1 egg.
- ½ std. cup bread crumbs. ⎫
- ½ std. cup grated cheese. ⎬ mix together
- ½ tsp. salt. ⎭
- butter or margarine for frying.

- Beat egg and milk together.
- Gently dip one slice of bread, at a time into this mixture.
- Coat well with bread crumb mixture.
- Melt butter or margarine in a frying pan. Fry each bread slice until both the sides are golden.
- Cut into cubes. Add to the soup just before serving.

'FLADCHEN' (PANCAKE STRIPS)

PREPARATION TIME : 15 MINUTES	COOKING TIME : 1 MIN. EACH

- 75 gms. plain flour.
- 1 egg.
- ½ level tsp. salt.
- 1 tsp. grated onion.
- 1 tbsp. chopped parsley or mint.
- 1 cup (150 ml.) water.
- butter or margarine for frying.

- Sieve together flour and salt in a bowl. Make a well in the centre, add egg gradually. Mix egg and flour.
- Add water a little at a time, mix well. The batter must be free from lumps.
- Add parsley and onion. Mix well.
- Heat frying pan, grease lightly, pour a tablespoon of batter, spread it well and make a thin pancake. Repeat with remaining batter in the same way.
- Cut them into thin strips and add to the soup as required.

'EIERTICH'

PREPARATION TIME : 10 MINUTES

COOKING TIME : 30 MINUTES

- 2 eggs.
- 1 cup (150 ml.) milk.
- a pinch of nutmeg.
- pinch of salt.
- foil.

- Place milk and eggs in a bowl and beat well until fluffy.
- Add salt and nutmeg. Mix well.
- Pour into a well greased square dish. Cover it with foil. Place it in another sauce pan with hot but not boiling water.
- Simmer gently over low heat, until Eiertich is firm.
- Unmould it, cut into cubes and add to the soup, just before serving.

SNOW BALLS

PREPARATION TIME : 10 MINUTES

COOKING TIME : 5 MINUTES

- 3 egg whites.
- 3 level tsps. castor sugar.
- pinch of salt.
- 1 tsp. lime juice.
- 1 level tsp. ground cinnamon.

- Beat egg whites until fluffy. Sprinkle lime juice and salt, beat until firm.
- Beat in sugar, a little at a time.
- Scoop into small balls and place on the boiling soup. Cover the sauce pan. Remove from heat. Leave to set for 5 minutes.
- Sprinkle with cinnamon before serving.

DUMPLINGS

- 1 cup (100 gms.) plain flour.
- 1 cup (150 ml.) milk.
- 2 eggs beaten.
- 1 tsp. butter or margarine.
- pinch of salt.
- pinch of nutmeg.

- Sieve flour and salt in a bowl.
- Heat milk in a sauce pan with butter or margarine and nutmeg. Bring to the boil.
- Remove from heat, add flour and beat vigorously until a smooth dough is formed.
- Add beaten eggs, beat again until smooth.
- Scoop off small dumplings with a wet spoon. Cook in boiling salted water first or put directly into the soup if dumplings are used for clear soup.

Herb Dumplings: Mix with the dumpling mixture at stage 4, 2 tablespoons each of mint and coriander.

CHEESE BALLS

- 1 cup (100 gms.) plain flour.
- 2 cups (300 ml.) milk.
- 1 egg.
- 1 tsp. butter or margarine.
- ½ cup (50 gms.) grated cheese.
- pinch of salt.
- pinch of nutmeg.

- Sieve flour and salt in a bowl.
- Heat milk, cheese, butter or margarine, and nutmeg in a sauce pan.
- Remove from heat, add flour and beat vigorously till a smooth dough is formed.
- Add beaten eggs, beat again until smooth.
- Scoop small amounts of the mixture with a wet spoon and cook in salted water to make dumplings. Add to the soup.

CONSOMMÉ 'A' LA JULIENNE
(CONSOMMÉ WITH VEGETABLES)

PREPARATION TIME : 3 - 4 HOURS	COOKING TIME : 10 MINUTES	SERVES : 4

- 5 cups/1 litre consommé (see page 6).
- 1 large carrot, peeled and shredded into matchsticks.
- 1 medium turnip peeled and shredded into matchsticks.
- 1 spring onion, shredded into matchsticks.
- 1 celery shredded into matchsticks.

- Prepare the vegetables and cook in boiling water until tender and drain.
- Divide vegetables into 4 parts and place at the bottom of 4 soup cups.
- Pour piping hot consommé into the soup cups. Serve as soon as possible.

Vegetarian Consommé 'A' La Julienne: Omit the consommé. Use 5 cups vegetable stock instead (see page 79).
Proceed as above.

CONSOMMÉ WITH TOMATOES

PREPARATION TIME : 3 - 4 HOURS	COOKING TIME : 1 HOUR	SERVES : 4 - 6

- 1 recipe consommé (see page 6).
- 500 gms. ripe tomatoes.
- 25 gms. vermicelli cooked.
- 2 level tsps. salt.
- ½ level tsp. pepper.
- 1 cup water.
- Mint for garnishing

- Wash, chop tomatoes. Place in a pan with water. Cook until tomatoes are pulpy. Stirring frequently, leave aside.
- Prepare the consommé as directed. Add tomatoes 15 minutes before the cooking time is completed. Add seasoning.
- Strain well.
- Place a little vermicelli in each soup cups and pour the hot consommé on top and serve hot, garnished with mint.

Vegetable Tomato Consommé: use 1 recipe vegetable stock in place of consommé and proceed as above.

SIMPLE CONSOMMÉ

PREPARATION TIME : 3 - 4 HOURS

COOKING TIME : 1 HOUR　　　**SERVES : 4**

- 5 cups basic bone stock.
- 3 whole black pepper corns.
- 2 egg whites half whisked.
- 2 egg shells washed and crushed.
- 100 gms lean meat finely chopped and washed.
- 1 level tsp. salt.
- 3 tbsps. sherry.

- Cool the stock and remove any fat.
- Place the stock in a pan, heat it slowly until nearly boiling.
- Add pepper corns, salt, egg shells, egg whites and meat.
- Bring the stock to the boil, whisking constantly with a fork or wire whisk.
- Cover and simmer over low heat for 1 hour and strain through a muslin cloth.
- Add the sherry (the soup should be a clear deep amber colour).

Note: A little meat extract can be added if necessary. Also can be made earlier and reheated.

COLD JELLIED CONSOMMÉ

PREPARATION TIME : ½ HOUR

COOKING TIME : 1 HOUR　　　**SERVES : 4**

- 1 recipe consommé. (see page 6).
- 6 trotters cleaned.
- ¼ tsp. ground nutmeg.
- 2 level tsps. salt.
- 2 bay leaves.
- 1 level tsp. red chilli powder.
- ½ level tsp. black pepper.
- 2 tbsps. finely chopped coriander for garnishing.
- lemon sliced.

- Wash the trotters well, cover them with boiling water, scrape off the hair from the trotters with a knife.
- Place consommé and trotters in a pan. Add salt, bay leaves, pepper, chilli powder and nutmeg and bring to boil. Reduce heat and simmer until tender.
- Remove the trotters. Allow to cool and set.
- Serve cold but not chilled. Garnish with coriander and lemon slices.

VEGETARIAN JELLIED CONSOMMÉ

PREPARATION TIME : 10 MINUTES

COOKING TIME : 2 HOURS   SERVES : 4

- 1 recipe consommé with tomatoes (see page 5).
- 1 tbsp. gelatine mixed with ½ cup hot water.
- 2 tbsp. finely chopped mint or parsley.
- 1 tbsp. sherry (optional).
- 1 tbsp. lemon juice.

- Prepare consommé as instructed.
- Add gelatine mixture. Stir well.
- Stir in lemon juice and optional sherry.
- Allow to cool in refrigerator.
- Beat well before serving.
- Serve in individual cocktail glasses. Garnish with mint or parsley.

FRENCH ONION SOUP

PREPARATION TIME : 1½ HOURS

COOKING TIME : 1 HOUR   SERVES : 4 - 6

- 500 gms. onions, peeled and thinly chopped.
- 1 recipe chicken stock.
- 50 gms. butter.
- 3 tsps. plain flour.
- 3 level tsps. salt.
- ½ level tsp. white pepper.
- ½ level tsp. mustard.
- 4 - 6 slices of french bread lightly toasted.
- 50 gms. grated cheese.
- ½ cup white wine.

- Melt butter in a pan, add chopped onions, salt, pepper and mustard. Cook over a very gentle heat, stirring till onion is browned.
- Add the flour, stir until smooth. Pour in stock and white wine and stirring constantly bring to the boil. Cover and simmer for 30 minutes.
- Place a slice of toasted bread at the bottom of each soup bowl. Sprinkle cheese on each toast. Carefully pour hot soup on the bread.
- Place the soup bowls under a hot grill until the cheese begins to brown. Serve immediately.

Vegetarian Onion Soup: Omit chicken stock and add vegetable stock instead and follow the recipe.

CHILLED VEGETABLE SOUP

PREPARATION TIME : 15 MINUTES
PLUS 3 HOURS CHILLING

COOKING TIME : 20 MINUTES   SERVES : 4

- 500 gms. cucumber, sliced with peel.
- 2 medium potatoes peeled and diced.
- 1 small onion sliced.
- ⅝ cup/95 ml. milk.
- 2½ cups/375 ml. water or stock.
- pinch of dry mustard.
- 2 level tsps. salt.
- ½ level tsp. pepper.
- 4 sprigs of parsley.

- Put all ingredients except milk in a pan with water or stock. Cook until tender over low heat.
- Pass everything through a sieve. Add milk and mix well.
- Chill 2-3 hours before serving. Garnish with parsley.

Note: This soup can also be served hot.

LEMON SOUP

PREPARATION TIME : 1½ HOURS

COOKING TIME : 15 MINUTES   SERVES : 4 - 6

- 5 cups/1 litre chicken stock or water with 2 chicken soup cubes.
- 3 tbsps. lemon juice.
- 1 tsp. lemon rind grated.
- 1 egg.
- 2 level tsps. salt.
- ½ level tsp. pepper.
- 2 tbsps. mint finely chopped.

- Heat stock.
- Beat together lemon juice, rind and egg.
- Add to the stock stirring constantly.
- Add salt and pepper.
- Serve cold or hot garnished with mint.

Vegetarian Lemon Soup:

Use vegetable stock in place of chicken stock and omit egg.

COLD CUCUMBER SOUP

PREPARATION TIME : 10 MINUTES, FREEZING TIME 30 MINUTES

COOKING TIME : 20 MINUTES   SERVES : 4 - 6

- 500 gms. cucumbers.
- 1 medium onion chopped.
- 1 tbsp. butter softened.
- 4¼ cups vegetable stock or water.
- ¾ cup milk.
- pinch of mustard.
- 2 tbsps. mint finely chopped.
- 2 level tsps. salt.
- ½ level tsp. pepper.
- lemon slices for garnishing.

- Roughly peel cucumbers and chop.
- Melt butter and fry onion. Add cucumber and half the stock. Simmer for 20 minutes.
- Remove and put through sieve.
- Add milk, remaining stock and seasoning to the puree.
- Pour into freezing tray, freeze for 30 minutes.
- Serve in individual soup bowls. Garnish with lemon slices.

CHILLED TOMATO SOUP

PREPARATION TIME : 30 MINUTES

COOKING TIME : 15 MINUTES   SERVES : 4

- 500 gms. tomatoes, washed and halved.
- ½ small beetroot.
- 1 medium onion chopped.
- 1 small piece celery chopped.
- ½ tsp. Worcestershire sauce.
- 1 tsp. lemon juice.
- 2 level tsps. salt.
- ½ level tsp. pepper.
- 1 bay leaf.
- 4½ cups water or stock.
- few lemon slices and mint sprigs for garnishing.

- Place all ingredients in a pan with water or stock and cook until the tomatoes are soft.
- Remove beetroot, rub remaining mixture through a sieve and pour into the freezing tray until slightly set.
- Serve in individual soup bowls garnished with lemon slices and mint.

Note: Canned tomato soup can be used instead of fresh tomatoes.

STRAWBERRY SOUP

PREPARATION TIME : 10 MINUTES & CHILLING TIME 6 HOURS

COOKING TIME : 25 MINUTES

SERVES : 4

- 1 kg. strawberries, cleaned and hulled.
- 2 medium apples, peeled cored and grated.
- 1 litre orange and apple juice or equal quantity of fruit juice and water.
- 25 gms. sugar.
- 3 tbsps. red wine (optional).
- 1 std. cup yoghurt.
- 2 tbsps. cornflour.
- juice of one small lime.

- Keep a few strawberries for garnishing.
- Put the remaining strawberries in a liquidiser or pass through a wire sieve. Make a puree.
- Place in a large pan strawberry puree, apple, all juices, sugar. Bring to the boil. Reduce heat and simmer another 10 minutes.
- Mix cornflour with little juice or water. Add this to the pan. Cook for further 5 minutes, stirring continuously.
- Add wine. Skim any froth from the surface of the soup.
- Cool and chill it thoroughly before serving.
- Serve in individual bowls. Garnish with sliced strawberries and 1 - 2 spoonfuls of yoghurt.

Note: Cream can be used in place of yoghurt.

Facing Page:

Onion Soup (page 7)

ABQUSHTE MIVEH
(IRANIAN DRYFRUIT SOUP)
An extremely healthy soup rich in vitamins and protein.

| PREPARATION TIME : 10 MINUTES | COOKING TIME : 2 HOURS | SERVES : 4 - 6 |

- 250 gms. lean lamb or any meat cut into small cubes.
- 2 onions chopped.
- 1 lime omani (dried lime).
- 1½ cups prunes pitted.
- 1 cup dried apricots pitted and halved.
- ½ cup chopped dried peaches.
- 2 tbsps. raisins.
- 1 tbsp. brown sugar (optional).
- 2 tbsps. ghee or butter.
- 8½ cups water.
- 2 tbsps. lemon juice.
- 2 level tsps. salt.
- ½ tsp. pepper.
- a pinch of turmeric

- Put meat cubes dried lime and water together in a sauce pan. Bring to the boil.
- Add salt and pepper. Cover and simmer for 1½ hours, until meat is almost tender. Remove dried lime.
- Heat ghee or butter in a fry pan. Fry onion until transparent. Add turmeric. Mix well. Cook until slightly brown.
- Wash all dry fruits and add to the soup. Cover and simmer for 30 minutes.
- Add lemon or lime juice and sugar. Stir well.
- Serve hot or cold, with almond rice (see page 1).

Vegetarian Abqushte Miveh:
Omit meat and proceed as above.

Facing Page:

Borsch (page 14)
Minestrone D'Asti Soup (page 16)
Slimmers Chowder (page 19)
Sunshine Slaw (page 44)

APPLE SOUP

PREPARATION TIME : 10 MINUTES   COOKING TIME : 20 MINUTES   SERVES : 4 - 6

- 1 kg. cooking apples, cored and chopped with peel.
- 1 litre water.
- $5/8$ cup 95 ml white wine (optional).
- 3 tbsps. lemon juice.
- pinch of salt.
- 1 tbsp. sugar.
- pinch of nutmeg.
- $1/2$ level tsp. cinnamon powder.
- lemon rings for garnishing.
- $1/2$ tsp. cardamom powder

- Place apples in a pan with water, salt, nutmeg, cinnamon powder and lemon juice. Simmer until tender, then rub through a sieve.
- Add white wine. Mix well.
- Add sugar while mixture is warm to dissolve well.
- Chill before serving. Garnish with lemon rings. Excellent for summer.

Variation:

Spiced apple soup: add 1 level teaspoon each ground roasted cumin, cinnamon, and $1/2$ level teaspoon cardamom powder to the apples while cooking.

Apple and orange soup: Add grated rind and juice of 2 oranges to the apples while cooking.

COLD CHERRY SOUP

PREPARATION TIME : 10 MINUTES PLUS 30 MINUTES   COOKING TIME : 20 MINUTES   SERVES : 4 - 6

- 500 gms. fresh or canned cherries.
- juice of 1 lemon.
- 1 tsp. lemon rind grated.
- sugar to taste.
- few mint leaves.
- 1 litre/5 cups water.

- Place cherries and water in a pan.
- Add lemon juice, rind and sugar.
- Gently cook over medium heat until tender.
- Remove a few cherries and keep aside for garnishing. Rub remaining cherries through a sieve. Pour into freezing tray. Freeze slightly for 30 minutes.
- Serve in individual soup bowls, garnished with cherries and mint.

VEGETABLE SOUP MILANESE

PREPARATION TIME : 20 MINUTES	COOKING TIME : 2½ HOURS	SERVES : 6 - 8

- ³/₄ cup white bean (haricot) soaked overnight.
- ½ cup rice, washed, soaked and drained.
- 2 cups shelled peas.
- 1 small cabbage shredded.
- 4 medium potatoes peeled and cubed.
- 2 large tomatoes blanched and chopped.
- 2 courgettes thinly sliced.
- 3 cloves garlic crushed.
- 2 stalks celery sliced.
- 3 medium carrots peeled and diced.
- 2 medium onions sliced.
- 2 sprigs parsley.
- 2 tbsps. chopped basil leaves.
- 2 tbsps. grated cheese.
- 3 level tsps. salt.
- 1 level tsp. pepper.
- 2 tbsps. margarine.
- 12 cups water.

- Boil beans in a deep pan with plenty of water (do not add salt) until cooked but firm. Drain well.
- Heat margarine in a pan. Saute onions and garlic until soft but not brown.
- Add beans and all vegetables except peas and cabbage. Fry for 10 minutes and pour in water.
- Add salt/pepper, lower heat and let it simmer for 1 hour 40 minutes.
- Add peas and cabbage and after 15 minutes, add rice and cook for a further 25 minutes.
- Add basil leaves and parsley before serving. Serve hot in individual soup bowls, topped with grated cheese.
- This soup can be served cold in summer.
- If you want a richer flavour add a few rashers of chopped bacon to the soup while cooking.

BEETROOT SOUP

PREPARATION TIME : ½ HOUR	COOKING TIME : 15 MINUTES	SERVES : 4 - 6

- 2 medium beetroots boiled, peeled and grated.
- 5 cups/1 litre vegetable stock or chicken stock.
- 2 tbsps. lemon juice.
- 2 level tsps. salt.
- ½ tsp. pepper.
- 1 lemon curl.
- 1 tbsp. mint leaves finely chopped.

- Heat the stock in a pan. Add lemon juice, lemon curl, beetroot and seasoning. Stir well. Cook for 5 minutes more. Remove lemon curl.
- Remove from fire. Serve hot, garnished with mint.

Note: Can also be served cold.

BORSCH

PREPARATION TIME : 25 MINUTES	COOKING TIME : 1½ HOURS	SERVES : 4 - 6

- 2 medium beetroots peeled and grated.
- 2 medium carrots pared and diced.
- 2 medium onions chopped.
- 4 large tomatoes blanched deseeded and chopped.
- 2 cloves garlic crushed.
- 1 small stick celery chopped.
- 1 tbsp. vinegar.
- 2 tbsps. sour cream or cream cheese.
- 2 level tsps. salt.
- ½ level tsp. pepper.
- 7 cups (1¾ litre) water or stock.

- Put beetroots, carrots, onions, celery, tomatoes and garlic in a pan with stock or water. Cover and simmer for 1½ hours.
- Add vinegar and seasoning.
- Serve hot garnished with sour cream and with salad accompaniment.

Note: Instead of sour cream you may garnish with Eiertich (see page 3).

FARMERS PEA SOUP

PREPARATION TIME : 10 MINUTES	COOKING TIME : 30 MINUTES	SERVES : 4

- 500 gms. fresh tender peas with pods, washed.
- 1 medium onion chopped.
- 1 tbsp. butter.
- 1 level tsp. sugar.
- 2 level tsps. salt.
- 1/2 level tsp. pepper.
- 5/8 cup/95 ml. milk.
- 5 cups/1 1/4 litre water.
- 2-3 sprigs mint.
- 1 cup bread croutons fried.
- 2 tbsps. mint, finely chopped.
- 2 tbsps. cream (optional).

- Place pea pods and water in a pan with onion, mint, seasoning, and simmer over medium heat until tender.
- Rub through a wire sieve vigorously so that the flesh of the pea pods are pushed through and only skins are left.
- Return to the pan, add butter and milk.
- If the soup becomes very thick, extra stock or milk can be added.
- Serve hot, garnished with croutons, cream and mint.

SIMPLE CARROT SOUP

PREPARATION TIME : 1 1/2 HOURS	COOKING TIME : 20 MINUTES	SERVES : 4 - 6

- 6 large carrots, peeled and grated.
- 4 cups chicken stock or vegetable stock.
- 1 1/4 cups/190 ml. milk.
- pinch of mustard.
- 2 level tsps. salt.
- 1/2 level tsp. pepper.
- pinch of sugar.
- 2 tbsps. parsley or mint finely chopped.

- Place carrots in a pan with stock and milk. Simmer over medium heat until cooked.
- Add salt, pepper, mustard and sugar.
- Pour into heated soup bowls. Garnish with parsley or mint.

Quick carrot soup:

Simply omit stock and use water instead. Follow recipe as above.

MINESTRONE D'ASTI

(VEGETABLE SOUP FROM ASTI (ITALY)

| PREPARATION TIME : 15 MINUTES | COOKING TIME : 1 HR. 50 MINS. | SERVES : 4 - 6 |

- 250 gms. fresh haricot beans shelled.
- 4 medium potatoes peeled and diced.
- 1/2 small cabbage finely shredded and washed.
- 2 medium carrots peeled and diced.
- 1 stalk celery chopped.
- 25 gms. thin noodles broken into tiny pieces or 25 gms. rice.
- 4 cloves garlic.
- 3 sprigs of parsley finely chopped.
- 12 leaves of basil finely chopped.
- 3 level tsps. salt.
- 1/2 level tsp. white pepper.
- 100 gms. grated cheese.
- 1 litre water.

- Put in a large pan beans and water together. Bring to the boil. Cook for 1 hour.
- Add potatoes, cabbage, celery, carrots and salt. Continue to cook for 35 minutes.
- Add noodles and cook for another 10-12 minutes. If using rice then 15 minutes.
- Grind basil, parsley and garlic to a paste and add to the soup. Dissolve the cheese with few spoons of soup. Mix well and pour the mixture into the soup. Stir well.
- Season with a little freshly ground white pepper and serve immediately.

Note: For better flavour use 2-3 rashers of chopped bacon to the soup. Traditionally, tiny thimble shaped ditalini noodles are used.

QUICK VEGETABLE CHOWDER

| PREPARATION TIME : 10 MINUTES | COOKING TIME : 30 MINUTES | SERVES : 4 |

- 1 pkt. vegetable soup.
- 2 medium potatoes peeled and diced.
- 150 gms. cheese grated.
- 2 tbsps. parsley or mint finely chopped.

- Prepare the soup as directed on packet.
- Bring it to boil, add potatoes. Cover and simmer for 20 minutes.
- Serve hot in individual soup bowls. Top with grated cheese and parsley.

SPRING ONION SOUP (NON-VEG.)

PREPARATION TIME : 10 MINUTES	COOKING TIME : 45 MINUTES	SERVES : 4 - 6

- 3 small spring onions sliced.
- 4 small carrots peeled and diced.
- 1 egg beaten.
- 1/2 small lettuce shredded.
- 1 1/2 tbsps. flour.
- 4 tbsps. milk.
- 2 tbsps. margarine.
- 5 cups white stock (see page 79).
- 2 level tsps. salt.
- 1/2 level tsp. black pepper.
- pinch of mustard.
- extra margarine.

- Keep a few spoons of sliced spring onion for garnishing.
- Heat margarine and lightly saute remaining onions, lettuce and carrots.
- Add stock and simmer for 35 minutes.
- Rub through a sieve and return to the pan.
- Mix flour, milk and all seasoning and add to the soup.
- Bring gently to the boil, stirring well. Remove from fire and stir in beaten egg.
- Heat extra margarine. Fry remaining sliced onions until golden brown.
- Serve hot, garnished with fried onion.

Vegetarian Spring Onion Soup:
Omit white stock and use water or vegetable stock instead. Omit egg. You may use 1/2 cup cream instead if desired and follow the remaining recipe as given above.

QUICK GREEN PEA SOUP

PREPARATION TIME : 10 MINUTES | **COOKING TIME : 10 MINUTES** | **SERVES : 4**

- 250 gms. green peas shelled.
- 4$^{1}/_{2}$ cups/1 litre water or vegetable stock.
- 1 onion chopped.
- 2 level tsps. salt.
- $^{1}/_{2}$ level tsp. pepper.
- 2 tbsps. cream or top of milk.
- 2 tbsps. mint or parsley finely chopped.

- Boil stock or water, add peas and onion. Cook for 10 minutes.
- Rub through a sieve, return to the pan.
- Add all remaining ingredients and mix well. Just before serving heat and serve hot.
- If you are using canned peas, cook only for 2 minutes.

ZUPPA - DI - CECI

(ITALIAN CHICK-PEA SOUP)

PREPARATION TIME : 20 MINUTES | **COOKING TIME : 3 HOURS** | **SERVES : 6**

- 1 cup chick peas soaked overnight.
- 100 gms. spinach cleaned and chopped.
- 2 medium onions chopped.
- 2 stalks of celery finely chopped.
- 3 medium carrots peeled and diced.
- 2 cloves.
- 1 bay leaf.
- 1 sprig sage.
- 4 tbsps. tomato paste or 6 tbsps. tomato puree.
- 1 cup white wine.
- 3 tbsps. parsley finely chopped.
- 3 level tsps. salt.
- $^{1}/_{2}$ level tsp. pepper.
- 1 level tsp. chilli powder.
- 2 tbsps. margarine.
- 10-11 cups water or vegetable stock.

- Bring chick peas to the boil with plenty of water. Cook until soft (do not add salt). Drain well.
- Melt margarine in a pan and saute onion until soft (not brown). Add celery.
- Add bay leaf, carrots, sage, cloves, salt, pepper, white wine and chilli powder. Mix well and pour in water or vegetable stock. Cover and simmer over low heat for 2 hours.
- Add chick peas, spinach and tomato paste. Cook for a further 25 minutes.
- Discard sage and serve hot, garnished with parsley.

SLIMMERS SPINACH SOUP

| PREPARATION TIME : 10 MINUTES | COOKING TIME : 35 MINUTES | SERVES : 4 - 6 |

- 500 gms. spinach, discard hard stems.
- 2 medium onion chopped.
- $5/8$ cup/95 ml. milk.
- 5 cups/$1^{1}/_4$ litre water.
- 3 level tsps. salt.
- $1/2$ level tsp. black pepper.
- pinch of grated nutmeg.

- Wash spinach and chop roughly. Place in a pan with water, onion and seasoning. Simmer until tender.
- Rub through a sieve. Add milk and grated nutmeg. Mix well and reheat.
- Serve hot.

Variation:

Tomato-Spinach Soup: use 5 cups tomato juice instead of water and follow the recipe as above.

SLIMMERS CHOWDER

| PREPARATION TIME : 20 MINUTES | COOKING TIME : 30 MINUTES | SERVES : 4 - 6 |

- 250 gms. cabbage shredded.
- 2 medium carrots.
- 2 small onions chopped.
- 3 large tomatoes blanched and chopped.
- 1 stick celery.
- 1 capsicum deseeded.
- 6 button mushrooms sliced.
- 5 cups water or stock.
- 2 tbsps. mint or parsley finely chopped for garnishing.
- 1 tbsp. margarine.
- $1/2$ tsp. yeast extract.

- Melt the margarine and fry chopped onions until soft.
- Add blanched tomatoes with all other vegetables, except cabbage.
- Pour in stock or water with yeast extract. Cover and simmer over low heat for 20 minutes.
- Stir in cabbage and cook for another 10 minutes.
- Garnish with chopped parsley. Serve hot.

ASPARAGUS SOUP

PREPARATION TIME : 10 MINUTES | COOKING TIME : 10 MINUTES | SERVES : 4

- 1 can asparagus soup.
- 2¹/₂ cups/375 ml. milk.
- 1 tbsp. cornflour.
- 1 tbsp. butter or margarine.
- seasoning as per taste.

- Open the asparagus can, drain and keep aside liquid from the can.
- Chop the asparagus into small pieces.
- Mix together milk and asparagus liquid.
- Heat butter or margarine, sprinkle cornflour and stir well. Pour milk mixture. Stir continuously to prevent lump formation. Add seasonings and stir.
- Add asparagus. Cook for 5 minutes. Serve hot with salad and accompaniment.

TOMATO AND NOODLE SOUP

COOKING TIME : 10 MINUTES | SERVES : 4

- 1 can - tomato soup.
- 1 can - vegetable soup.
- ¹/₂ cup broken noodles.

- Mix both the soups and heat.
- Add noodles.
- Simmer gently for 10 minutes.
- Serve hot with accompaniment and salad.

CHICKEN AND MUSHROOM SOUP

COOKING TIME : 10 MINUTES

- 1 can chicken soup.
- 1 can mushroom soup.
- 4 rasher bacon chopped.
- 1 onion chopped.

- Mix both the soups.
- Saute bacon until crisp. Remove. Fry onion in the bacon fat until transparent.
- Pour into soup mixture, mix well. Serve hot, garnished with fried bacon.

Vegetarian:
Omit chicken soup and bacon. Use 1 can of tomato soup and chopped parsley to garnish.

CARROT AND CORIANDER SOUP

PREPARATION TIME : 10 MINUTES

MAKES 3 CUPS

- 1 cup boiled and mashed carrot.
- ½ cup chopped coriander leaves.
- 2 cups water.
- 1 tbsp. lemon juice.
- seasoning.

- Put all ingredients in a liquidiser for 1-2 minutes.
- Heat the mixture serve hot with bread and flavoured butter (see page 72).

COCONUT AND PUMPKIN SOUP
(THAILAND)

PREPARATION TIME : 20 MINUTES	COOKING TIME : 30 MINUTES	SERVES : 4 - 5

- 500 gms. pumpkin.
- 1 cup (150 ml.) thick coconut milk (see page 82).
- 4 cups (600 ml.) thin coconut milk (see page 82).
- ½ std. cup dried shrimps ⎫
- 3 shallots. ⎪ Ground
- 2 fresh red chillies. ⎬ to a
- 2 fresh green chillies. ⎪ paste
- 1½ tsps. shrimp paste. ⎭
- 3 tsps. lime juice.
- 6 sweet basil leaves.
- 2 cups 300 ml. water.
- 2 level tsps. salt.

- Roughly peel the pumpkin. Leave little peel to prevent the flesh breaking and cut into large pieces. Sprinkle lemon juice.
- Place thick coconut milk in a sauce pan. Bring to the boil. Add ground paste and mix well. Cook for 5 minutes.
- Add pumpkin, reduce heat, cook for 10 minutes. Pour in half of thin coconut milk and salt. Cook until pumpkin is tender but not soft.
- Add remaining coconut milk, water and basil leaves. Stir well. Bring to the boil.
- Serve hot.

JAPANESE FISH BROTH

PREPARATION TIME : 15 MINUTES	COOKING TIME : 30 MINUTES	SERVES : 4 - 6

- 500 gms. head trimmings and bones of any fish.
- 1½ litres water.
- 1 tsp. grated fresh ginger.
- 1 spring onion.
- 1 tsp. soya sauce.
- 1 tbsp. sake or dry sherry.
- 2 level tsps. salt.
- extra sliced spring onion for garnishing.

- Place fish head, trimmings and bones, in a sauce pan with ginger, water and spring onion. Bring to the boil, then reduce heat and simmer. Skim the surface.
- Cook for 20 minutes. Cool and strain into a clean pan.
- Add soya sauce, sake or wine and salt.
- Serve hot, garnished with spring onion.

Note: Traditionally a thin slice of raw fish is put in each bowl and boiling broth poured over.

THAI CHICKEN SOUP

- 50 gms. cellophane noodles.
- 4 black chinese mushrooms or
- 1 cup sliced button mushrooms.
- 150 gms. cooked and ground chicken or meat.
- 50 gms. bean curd (toffu).
- 1 egg.
- 4 spring onions sliced.
- 2 cloves garlic.
- 5 whole black peppers.
- 2 tbsps. chopped bamboo shoots.
- 1 tsp. chopped coriander root.
- 1 tsp. salt.
- 1½ litres chicken stock (see page 79).
- 2 tbsps. finely chopped coriander leaves.

- Wash and soak mushrooms in hot water for 30 minutes. Discard hard stems and slice the caps, if using canned mushrooms, then wash thoroughly and slice.
- Soak noodles in hot water until soft. Drain and keep aside.
- Put together garlic, pepper, coriander root and grind to a paste.
- Mix the paste and ground chicken or meat together and make a dough. Take a teaspoon in your palm at a time and shape into small balls.
- Heat stock in a large sauce pan. Bring to the boil, add chicken or meat balls. Reduce heat and simmer for 25 minutes.
- Add noodles, salt, mushrooms, bamboo shoot. Cook for another 10 - 15 minutes.
- Add bean curd and spring onion. Cook for a further 5 minutes.
- Whisk egg lightly and add to the soup. Stir continuously until egg looks like threads.
- Serve hot garnished with the chopped coriander.

Vegetarian Thai Chicken Soup:
Omit egg. Use 150 gms. of cooked soya mince instead of chicken or meat and proceed as above.

SZECHWAN SOUP

PREPARATION TIME : 30 MINUTES	COOKING TIME : 30 MINUTES	SERVES : 4

- 6 dried chinese mushrooms soaked in hot water for ½ hour.
- 2 cups soaked cellophane noodles.
- ½ cup meat finely chopped.
- ½ cup prawns cooked and finely chopped.
- ½ cup fresh bean curd (toffu) chopped.
- 2 eggs beaten.
- 2 tbsps. oil.
- 2 tbsps. soya sauce.
- 2 level tsps. sugar.
- ½ cup hot water.
- 1 tbsps. mild vinegar.
- 1 tbsp. dry sherry.
- 1 tsp. chilli oil (see page 82).
- 1½ tbsps. cornflour. ⎫ mix
- 6 tbsps. cold water. ⎭ together
- 3 level tsps. salt.
- ½ level tsp. pepper.
- 1 litre stock or water.

- Cut off and discard stems from mushrooms and slice thinly.
- Cut soaked noodles into 2" lengths.
- Heat oil, in a large sauce pan, fry mushrooms and meat, stirring well, until colour turns light brown.
- Add sugar, ½ cup hot water and soya sauce. Simmer over low heat.
- Add prawns, stock and noodles. Simmer for 5 minutes.
- Add bean curd, vinegar, chilli oil and sherry.
- Dribble beaten eggs into simmering soup. Stir constantly so that egg separates into fine shreds.
- Add cornflour mixture. Stir well and simmer until the soup is thickened.
- Add salt and pepper.
- Serve hot.

BEER SOUP

| PREPARATION TIME : 5 MINUTES | COOKING TIME : 30 MINUTES | SERVES : 4 - 6 |

- 4 cups (1 litre) beer.
- 3 cups (450 ml.) milk.
- 2 x 1" pieces cinnamon.
- 50 gms. sugar (optional).
- 1 tsp. lemon juice.
- 2 egg yolks with 2 tbsps. cold water.
- 3 level tbsps. cornflour ⎱ mix
- ½ cup (75 ml.) water.   ⎰ together
- snow balls for garnishing (see page 3)
- 2½ cups water.

- Mix together water, cinnamon and milk. Bring to the boil. Remove from heat.
- Gently stir in the cornflour mixture. Return to the heat and bring to the boil.
- Add beer, lemon juice and sugar. Cook for a few minutes but do not boil.
- Beat egg yolks with water and add to the soup, stirring continuously over low heat for a few minutes. Do not boil.
- Serve hot or cold, topped with snow balls.

WHITE WINE SOUP

(TO GIVE YOU ENERGY WHEN YOU ARE TIRED)

| PREPARATION TIME : 5 MINUTES | COOKING TIME : 30 MINUTES | SERVES : 4 - 5 |

- 4 cups (1 lit.) white wine or cider.
- 2 cups (300 ml.) water.
- 2 x 1" pieces cinnamon.
- 1 tsp. lemon essence.
- 35 gms. cornflour.
- 4 tbsps. cold water.
- 2 tbsps. sugar.
- 2 egg yolks with 2 tbsps. cold water.

- Put water, cinnamon and lemon essence in a sauce pan. Bring to boil. Remove from heat.
- Mix cornflour with water and stir into the boiled water. Return to the heat, bring to boil again.
- Add wine and sugar, lower heat. Do not boil.
- Beat egg yolks with water and add to the soup. Stir well.
- If you wish to serve the soup cold reduce the cornflour. Use only 25 - 30 gms.

ALMOND SOUP

A HIGHLY NUTRITIOUS SOUP RICH IN PROTEIN. EXCELLENT FOR GROWING CHILDREN.

PREPARATION TIME : 10 MINUTES	COOKING TIME : 17 MINUTES	SERVES : 4 - 6

- 100 gms. almonds blanched, ground with a little water.
- 1 medium onion chopped.
- 1 clove garlic crushed.
- 1 tbsp. finely chopped mint or parsley.
- 6 cups water or chicken stock (see page 79).
- 1 tbsp. fine bread crumbs.
- 2 level tsps. salt.
- ½ level tsp. pepper.
- few drops almond essence.
- 2 tbsps. butter or margarine.

- Heat butter or margarine. Fry onion and garlic till transparent but not brown.
- Sprinkle bread crumbs. Mix well.
- Add ground almond paste. Stir well.
- Pour in water or stock. Cover and simmer for 15 minutes.
- Add seasoning.
- Serve hot or cold. Garnish with chopped mint or parsley.

Note: For chicken stock, bouillon cubes can be used.

Vegetarian Almond Soup: Omit chicken stock and use vegetable stock or water. Proceed as given below.

Facing Page:
Almond Soup (page 26)

HOT BUTTERMILK SOUP

EXCELLENT FOR SLIMMERS SPECIALLY FOR COMPLEXION.

| PREPARATION TIME : 10 MINUTES | COOKING TIME : 15 MINUTES | SERVES : 4 - 5 |

- 5 cups (750 ml.) buttermilk
- 4 level tbsps. chick pea flour (besan).
- 1 tbsp. sugar (optional).
- 2 level tsps. fenugreek seeds.
- ¾ tsp. black mustard seed.
- ½ tsp. cumin seeds.
- 4 dry red chillies.
- 10 curry leaves.
- 1 tsp. grated fresh ginger.
- 2 fresh green chillies chopped.
- 2 level tsps salt.
- 2 tbsps. margarine or oil.
- 2 tbsps. finely chopped fresh coriander leaves.

- Mix chick pea flour with 1 cup buttermilk until smooth. Pour in remaining buttermilk.
- Heat margarine or oil, fry mustard and cumin seed and as they pop up and splatter, add red chillies, fenugreek, curry leaves, ginger, green chillies, salt and sugar. Stir well and fry until ingredients begin to brown.
- Pour in buttermilk mixture. Stir well and cook until slightly thickened.
- Serve hot, garnished with coriander.

Cold Buttermilk Soup:
Chill thoroughly before serving.

Facing Page:

Apple Soup (page 12)
Salad Nicoise (page 49)

SPANISH GAZPACHO

(ORIGINATED AS A SIMPLE PEASANT DISH WITH RAW VEGETABLES POUNDED BY HAND).

PREPARATION TIME : ½ HOUR + 6 - 8 HOURS CHILLING

NO COOKING

SERVES : 4 - 6

- 500 gms. tomatoes blanched, seeded and chopped.
- 2 medium onions chopped.
- 3 cloves garlic chopped.
- 1 medium cucumber peeled and chopped.
- 1 green capsicum seeded and chopped.
- 25 gms. almonds blanched and chopped (optional).
- 2 tbsps. chopped mint.
- 2 tbsps. chopped parsley.
- 2 tbsps. olive oil.
- 1 tbsp. wine vinegar (see page 82).
- 2 level tsps. salt.
- 1 level tsp. ground white pepper.
- 1 litre cold water.

For garnishing
- 1 cup peeled and diced cucumber.
- 1 large onion chopped.
- 1 red or green capsicum diced.
- 10 olives stoned and sliced. ice cubes.

- Put all ingredients together in a blender, except water. Blend at the lowest speed for 1 - 2 minutes until smooth.
- Pour into a large bowl and add water. Mix well. Cover and chill for 6 - 8 hours.
- Stir well before serving. Serve in individual bowls with ice cubes.
- Garnish ingredients can be served separately in individual bowls or added to the soup directly.
- If you want your gazpacho a little spicy add chopped green chillies.

MELOKHIA

(EGYPTIAN HERB SOUP) POPULAR AMONG RICH AND POOR ALIKE.

PREPARATION TIME : 15 MINUTES	COOKING TIME : 3½ HOURS	SERVES : 4 - 6

For Melokhia Stock :

- 1.2 kg. broiler chicken.
- 500 gms. tomatoes blanched and chopped.
- 2 medium onions chopped.
- 1 stick celery with leaves chopped.
- ½ tsp. freshly ground pepper.
- 1 tsp. salt.
- 10 cups / 2½ litres water.

For Melokhia Soup:

- 350 gms. fresh spinach washed and chopped.
- 6 cloves garlic.
- 1 tsp. ground coriander powder.
- ½ tsp. salt.
- pinch of red chilli powder.
- 2 tbsps. melted butter or margarine.
- 1 cup boiled rice.

- Place all the stock ingredients in a large pot. Bring to the boil; reduce heat. Cover and simmer for 3 hours. Skim time to time.
- Remove the chicken, strain the liquid and return the stock to the pot.
- Debone the chicken and cut up the meat and keep aside.
- Bring stock to the boil, add spinach. Simmer for 15 minutes. Stir and add boiled rice.
- Mix together crushed garlic and salt.
- Heat butter or margarine in a pan and fry garlic mixture until golden brown.
- Add coriander, chilli powder and mix. Add to the soup and mix well.
- Serve hot with cut chicken pieces.

Note: Melokhia is a herb traditionally used fresh or dried but spinach is used as a substitute, specially in India.

Vegetarian Melokhia: Simply omit chicken and use vegetable stock instead.

HARIRA WITH CHICKEN & LAMB
(MOROCCAN SOUP)

DURING RAMADAN (RAMZAN) HARIRA IS MADE WITH ONLY CHICK PEA WITHOUT MEAT IN MANY HOMES. HARIRA IS QUITE SIMILAR TO INDIAN HALEEM (HYDERABAD).

PREPARATION TIME : 20 MINUTES

COOKING TIME : 2 HOURS   **SERVES : 4 - 6**

- 1 kg. lean lamb or mutton, cut into large cubes.
- 1 kg. broiler chicken cut into 6 pieces.
- 500 gms. ripe tomatoes blanched and chopped roughly.
- 100 gms. chick peas soaked overnight.
- 2 large onions chopped.
- 4 cloves garlic crushed.
- 100 gms. lentil washed.
- 3 tbsps. rice washed and drained.
- 3 eggs beaten.
- juice of one lemon or lime.
- 2 green chillies chopped.
- 2 dry red chillies.
- 2 level tsps. salt.
- 1½ level tsps. turmeric powder.
- 1 level tsp. coriander powder.
- ½ level tsp. dry ginger powder.
- 1 level tsp. cinnamon powder.
- 4 tbsps. chopped parsley.
- lemon wedges.
- ½ cup (75 ml.) oil.
- 1 tsp. pepper.

- Heat oil in a large pan. Fry meat cubes until all sides turn light brown. Drain and keep aside.
- Fry chicken, onion, red chillies, garlic one by one and keep aside. Add chick peas. Fry for 5 - 8 minutes and add chicken with onion, meat cubes and garlic.
- Pour in water to cover the chicken, chick peas and other ingredients. Stir well.
- Add tomatoes, all ground spices and lentil, bring to the boil, reduce heat and simmer for 1 hour.
- Add rice and parsley. Cook for 30 minutes.
- Remove chicken pieces from soup and remove meat from bone and put the chicken meat back in the pot.
- Add salt, pepper and green chillies. Reduce heat and simmer again for 15 minutes.
- Beat together lemon juice and eggs.
- Pour it into the soup, stirring well.
- Serve immediately with lemon wedges and green salad.
- If you are not using chillies, then chilli sauce can be served separately.

Vegetarian Harira: Omit meat, chicken and eggs. Add 500 gms. cooked and fried soya nuggets instead. Use beaten yoghurt or cream for garnishing just before serving. Follow the remaining recipe as given above.

CALDO GALLECO (SPAIN)

| PREPARATION TIME : 20 MINUTES | COOKING TIME : 2½ HOURS | SERVES : 4 - 6 |

- 500 gms. potatoes.
- 250 gms. cabbage.
- 250 gms. dried haricot beans (soaked overnight).
- 2 medium onion, chopped roughly.
- 6 cloves garlic chopped.
- 2 turnips chopped with leaves.
- 2 - 3 rashers bacon.
- 150 gms. smoked meat.
- 3 level tsps. salt.
- ½ level tsp. pepper.
- 100 gms. small sausages.
- water.
- 2 tbsps. chopped mint.

- Place beans in a large sauce pan with enough water to cover them. Bring to the boil; cook until soft.
- Add onion, garlic, sausages, meat, bacon and simmer for 1 hour over low heat.
- Add cabbage, turnips and potatoes and boiling water if necessary. Add salt and pepper.
- Cover and simmer gently for another 1½ hours till flavour improves and vegetables start to disintegrate.
- Remove bacon rashers.
- Garnish with mint and serve hot with garlic bread.

Vegetarian Caldo Galleco:
- Omit bacon, meat and sausages.
- Use 500 gms. cooked soya nuggets instead and proceed as above.

SCOTCH BROTH

PREPARATION TIME : 20 MINUTES	COOKING TIME : 33 MINUTES	SERVES : 4

- 500 gms. lamb meat, washed, cleaned and fat removed.
- 2 medium onions chopped.
- 2 cloves garlic.
- 25 gms. pearl barley.
- 2 medium carrots pared and diced.
- 1 turnip pared and diced.
- 2 level tsps. salt.
- ½ level tsp. ground pepper.
- 2 tbsps. chopped parsley.
- 1½ litres water.

- Cut meat into small cubes.
- Place together water, meat, barley and seasonings in a pressure cooker. Cook for 25 minutes over low heat.
- Reduce the pressure, open lid and skim any fat off the surface of the soup.
- Add the diced vegetables and pressure cook for 8 minutes. Remove.
- Serve hot garnished with parsley.

Vegetarian Scotch Broth:
Use 1 cup cooked red kidney beans instead of meat and proceed as above.

SOPA-DE-AJO
(SPANISH GARLIC SOUP)

(EXCELLENT REMEDY FOR HIGH BLOOD PRESSURE. KEEPS CHOLESTEROL LEVEL LOW; ALSO FOR JOINT PAIN. GARLIC PROTECTS FROM MANY VIRAL DISEASES).

PREPARATION TIME : 10 MINUTES	COOKING TIME : 20 MINUTES	SERVES : 4 - 6

- 2 large pods garlic skinned and crushed.
- 125 ml. / ½ cup olive oil.
- 6 tomatoes blanched and chopped.
- 2 eggs beaten.
- 1 litre vegetables stock (see page 79) or water.
- 6 medium slices day old bread, cut into small squares.
- 2 tbsps. finely chopped mint.
- salt to taste.

- Heat oil in a sauce pan. Fry crushed garlic, add bread pieces, stir well. Cook until golden but not brown.
- Add stock or water, tomatoes and salt. Simmer for 10 minutes. The bread should not disintegrate.
- Stir in beaten eggs, just before serving and top with chopped mint.

KIDNEY BEAN SOUP WITH HERB DUMPLINGS

| PREPARATION TIME : 1 HOUR | COOKING TIME : 40 MINUTES | SERVES : 4 - 6 |

- 500 gms. red kidney beans.
- 1 large onion chopped.
- 2 sticks celery trimmed and diced.
- 2 small carrots peeled and diced.
- 25 gms. butter or margarine.
- 2 level tsps. salt.
- ½ level tsp. pepper.
- ½ tsp. thyme.
- 1½ litres vegetable stock or water (see page 79).
- 10 herb dumplings (see page 4).
- 2 level tbsps. cornflour.
- ½ cup milk.

- Soak red kidney beans overnight and cook in water (1½ litres) until soft. Reserve.
- Prepare dumplings cooked in salted water. Drain well and keep aside.
- Heat butter or margarine in a pan. Stir fry vegetables for sometime. Add water and cook. When cooked add vegetables to the kidney bean, with all seasoning.
- Sieve or liquidise the soup.
- Mix cornflour with milk. Add to the soup with dumplings. Simmer gently for a further 15 - 20 minutes.
- Serve hot.

LOBSTER CHOWDER

PREPARATION TIME : 20 MINUTES	COOKING TIME : 20 MINUTES	SERVES : 4 - 6

- 1 medium lobster cleaned, shelled and diced.
- 2 medium potatoes, boiled, peeled and diced.
- 1 medium onion, chopped.
- 2 rashers bacon, remove rind.
- 2 level tbsps. flour.
- 1 cup (150 ml.) milk.
- 1 level tsp. sugar.
- 3 level tsps. salt.
- ½ level tsp. black pepper powder.
- 6 cups (1½ litres) water.
- 2 tbsps. margarine.

- Wash and clean lobster shell well and place in a pan with water. Bring to the boil. Lower heat and simmer for 20 minutes.
- Strain and add enough water to make 1½ litres again.
- Cut bacon into thin strips.
- Heat margarine in a pan, fry bacon, add onion, stir well, fry until transparent. Then sprinkle flour over it. Stirring constantly, cook but do not allow to brown.
- Gently add the lobster stock. Stir well. Bring to boil gradually.
- As sauce begins to thicken, add lobster pieces with all other ingredients.
- Place the pan over boiling water or put in double saucepan. Cook until it forms a thick creamy mixture.
- Serve hot with accompaniments.

Vegetarian Lobster Chowder:

Use equal amounts of cooked soya nugget or vegetarian chicken (see basic in book 'The Flavours of China') and proceed as above.

SHAURBAT ADAS
(THIS SOUP COMES FROM THE ARAB STATES)

| PREPARATION TIME : 15 MINUTES | COOKING TIME : 1 HR. 25 MINS. | SERVES : 4 - 6 |

- 225 gms. red or black lentils.
- 2 medium onions chopped.
- 2 medium carrots diced.
- 2 medium onions sliced.
- 4 cloves garlic crushed roughly.
- 1 tsp. cumin powder.
- 2 level tsps. salt.
- ½ level tsp. pepper.
- juice of 1 lemon or lime.
- 2 litres chicken stock or water.
- ½ cup (75 ml.) olive oil.
- lemon wedges.
- 2 tbsps. finely chopped fresh mint.

- Wash and place lentils in a large saucepan or pot with stock or water. Add chopped onion and carrot. Bring to the boil. Reduce heat. Cover and simmer for 1 hour.
- Pass the mixture through a wire sieve or put in a liquidiser.
- Return to the saucepan. Add lemon juice, cumin, salt, pepper. Stir well and simmer again for 20 minutes and add more stock or water if necessary.
- Heat oil in a frying pan, saute garlic for 1 - 2 minutes. Remove from oil and fry sliced onion in the same oil until golden brown.
- Serve the soup in individual soup bowls; top each one with mint, fried garlic, onion, lemon wedges. Serve extra lemon juice separately.
- Serve with fresh green salad and garlic bread.

ZUPPA-DI-COZZE (ITALIAN MUSSEL SOUP)

PREPARATION TIME : 15 MINUTES

COOKING TIME : 40 MINUTES   **SERVES : 4 - 5**

- 1 kg. mussel.
- 500 gms. tomatoes blanched and chopped or ½ kg. tomato paste.
- 2 medium onions grated.
- 3 cloves garlic crushed.
- 1 small celery stalk chopped.
- 1 tsp. dried basil.
- ½ tsp. dried oregano.
- ½ level tsp. pepper.
- ¼ tsp. red chilli powder.
- 2 level tsps. salt.
- 150 ml. dry white wine (optional).
- 2 tbsps. finely chopped parsley.
- 1.25 litres water.
- 50 ml. olive oil.

- Wash mussels carefully until no trace of sand remains. Scrape them with a sharp knife and remove their beards.
- Heat oil in a large saucepan, fry onions, garlic and celery for a few minutes but do not brown. Stir in all seasonings and herbs. Cook for 1 minute.
- Add tomato paste mixed with a little water or blanched tomatoes.
- Pour over the water and wine. Simmer over low heat for 10 minutes.
- Add mussels, shaking the pan occasionally. Cook for another 15 minutes until the shells open. Discard any shells that do not open.
- Transfer the mussels from the pan and remove the top shell and keep hot.
- Strain the soup and pass the vegetables through a wire sieve and return the strained soup to the pan and bring to the boil.
- Add mussels and cook for a few minutes.
- Serve hot garnished with parsley.

Vegetarian Zuppa-di-Cozze:

Omit mussels. Use 500 gms. Indian cottage cheese or toffu cut into cubes. Add at stage 8 and proceed as above.

FISH BISQUE

PREPARATION TIME : 20 MINUTES	COOKING TIME : 40 MINUTES	SERVE : 4 - 6

- 500 gms. pomfret or any white fish.
- 2 medium onions chopped.
- 2 medium carrots pared and diced.
- juice of 1 lemon or lime.
- 1 egg yolk.
- 100 gms. butter or margarine.
- 4 tbsps. dry white wine.
- 3 tbsps. brandy.
- 2 tbsps. flour.
- 4 tbsps. double cream.
- 2 level tsps. salt.
- ½ level tsp. pepper.
- bouquet garni.
- 1 litre water.
- 2 tbsps. chopped parsley or mint.

- Wash fish in salted water. Drain, debone and cut into cubes and keep aside.
- Heat 2 tablespoons butter or margarine. Fry onions till transparent and add carrots. Saute for 10 minutes.
- Flambe brandy in a large spoon and pour on the vegetable. When the flavour has died, add fish.
- Pour in water and wine. Add bouquet garni tied in a muslin cloth. Cover and simmer gently over low heat for 30 minutes.
- Discard bouquet garni bag.
- Melt remaining butter or margarine. Stir in the flour. Cook for 1 minute stirring well.
- Gently pour the soup over the mixture, stirring well, bring to the boil. Simmer for 5 minutes.
- Add lime juice and seasoning.
- Mix together egg yolk and cream and add a little soup. Mix well and pour into the soup, stirring well.
- Do not boil while reheating.
- Transfer to a soup tureen. Garnish with lemon slices and parsley or mint.
- Serve hot with dinner rolls and salad.

Vegetarian Bisque:

Use mock fish (see page 75) instead of fish and follow the recipe as given above.

CHICKEN BROTH WITH RICE

PREPARATION TIME : 20 MINUTES | COOKING TIME : 3½ HOURS | SERVES : 4

- 1 kg. chicken.
- 1 cup (100 gms) rice washed and drained.
- 500 gms. mixed vegetables (carrots, peas, cauliflower, brussel sprouts, french beans etc.) cut into small pieces.
- 250 gms. new potatoes peeled and diced.
- 1 litre water.
- 2 level tsps. salt.
- 2 tbsps. finely chopped parsley.
- extra water.

- Clean and cut chicken into small pieces.
- Boil water and salt in a heavy bottom sauce pan. Add cut chicken with neck, heart and gizzard. Simmer gently over low heat until cooked.
- Remove them from broth. Add rice and vegetables. Cook until done.
- Add chicken liver. Cook for 2 minutes.
- Dice the cooked chicken and add to the soup. Mix well. Cook for a few minutes more and remove.
- Add extra water if needed.
- Serve hot garnished with parsley.

Vegetarian Broth with Rice:

Use 250 gms. cooked soya nuggets instead of chicken. Follow the above recipe but omit stage 4 and 5.

ZUPPA DI PESCE (ITALIAN FISH SOUP)

PREPARATION TIME : 40 MINUTES	COOKING TIME : 40 MINUTES	SERVES : 4 - 6

- 1 kg. assorted fish.
- 500 gms. ripe tomatoes blanched, seeded and chopped.
- 2 medium onions finely chopped.
- 2 cloves garlic crushed.
- 2 sprigs parsley finely chopped.
- ½ cup dry white wine.
- ⁴/₅ cup / 120 ml. olive oil or any oil.
- 3 level tbsps. salt.
- ½ level tsp. pepper.
- 1 - 2 level tsps ground dry chilli powder.
- 4 - 6 slices bread, fried.
- water.

- Clean and wash fish in plenty of salted water. Pat dry, cut off the heads. Cut the large fish into pieces.
- Place all fish wads in a pan with enough water to cover and 1 teaspoon salt. Bring to the boil and simmer gently.
- Heat oil in a large pan, fry onion, garlic and parsley till golden.
- Add tomatoes, stir well and pour in the wine and cook until thickened.
- Pour in ½ cup fish stock, all seasoning and cut fish. Stir well and cook for 20 minutes.
- Add remaining fish stock and simmer for 15 minutes more.
- Place a slice of fried bread in each soup bowl. Pour over the fish and stock. Serve hot.

BREAD AND CHEESE SOUP

PREPARATION TIME : 15 MINUTES	COOKING TIME : 30 MINUTES	SERVES : 4

- 2 French breads, sliced and toasted.
- 500 gms. cheese sliced.
- 2½ litres / 10 cups vegetable stock (see page 79).
- 2 tbsps. finely chopped parsley.

- Place alternate layers of toast and cheese in a large earthenware bowl or soup tureen.
- Bring stock to boil and immediately pour over the toast and cheese.
- Put in a warm oven 250°F, (120°C). Gas mark ¼ for 10 minutes before serving.
- Garnish with parsley.

SOPA-DE-ELOTE
(MEXICAN CORN SOUP)

PREPARATION TIME : 20 MINUTES	COOKING TIME : 1 HOUR	SERVES : 4 - 6

- 4 fresh baby corn cobs.
- 4 large tomatoes blanched and chopped.
- 1 large onion chopped.
- 3 cloves garlic crushed.
- ½ tsp. oregano.
- 1 level tsp. salt.
- 1 level tsp. red chilli powder (optional).
- 2 tsps. butter.
- ⅖ cup (60 ml.) single cream.
- 5 cups (1.25 litres) white stock (see page 79).
- 2 tbsps. finely chopped parsley or mint.

- Remove corn kernels from cobs by scrapping cobs with a spoon, discard cobs.
- Take half the corn kernels and make a puree in a liquidiser. Keep aside.
- Grind together salt and garlic to make a paste.
- Heat butter, add onion and garlic paste. Cook until translucent, but not browned.
- Add tomatoes, mash with back of a wooden spoon. Cook for 15 minutes.
- Pour in stock, stir well and add pureed corn and whole corn kernels, oregano, chilli powder and bring to boil. Reduce heat. Cover and simmer for 35 minutes.
- Slowly stir in cream. Serve hot. Pour into individual soup bowls. Garnish with parsley or mint.

Note: Tinned corn can be used if fresh corn is not available.

Vegetarian Sopa-De-Elote:

Omit white stock. Use vegetable stock or water instead and proceed as given above.

TEN WAYS TO MAKE QUICK SALADS

1. Pear and Cheese Salad:

Fill the halved canned pear with grated cheese or Indian cottage cheese crumbled and mixed with mayonnaise; garnish with grated fresh ginger, mixed with lemon juice.

2. Lettuce and Onion Salad:

Clean, wash, dry lettuce leaves. Break them into pieces. Add onion rings, sprinkle with lemon juice and a little chilli powder.

3. Cheese & Pineapple Salad:

Mix diced canned pineapple with diced cheese. Toss with lemon mayonnaise (see page 83). Pile on crisp lettuce.

4. Bean Sprout and Mushroom Salad:

Clean, wash, drain well bean sprouts. Mix with sliced canned button mushrooms, stem removed, dressed with hot Mexican dressing (see page 87). Garnish with onion rings.

5. For a quick Salad Platter:

Take raw cauliflower flowerettes, shredded cabbage, capsicum slices, carrot sticks, turnip slices, nuts, apples and banana sprinkled with lemon juice, grapes etc., each tossed individually in mustard dressing (see page 90).

6. Cabbage Salad:

Shredded white or red cabbage, chopped nuts and onion toss in white salad cream (see page 89). Serve in salad bowl, garnish with tomato wedges.

7. Apple, Grape and Carrot Salad:

Dried apple and carrots mixed with lemon juice tossed in orange mayonnaise (see page 85) or orange dressing (see page 89). Serve on a bed of lettuce Garnish with grapes.

8. Beetroot and Dill Salad:

Cooked, peeled and diced beetroots. Garnish with finely chopped dill or mint. Toss in garlic French dressing (see page 88).

9. Cucumber Salad:

Put together slices of cucumber, onions and tomatoes. Toss in apple juice dressing (see page 89). Garnish with finely chopped fresh coriander.

10. Carrot and Raisin Salad:

Mix 2 cups grated carrots with 2/3 cup seedless raisin. Toss in basic French dressing (see page 88).

ARTICHOKE CHICKEN SALAD

PREPARATION TIME : 45 MINUTES

COOKING TIME : 20 - 25 MINUTES   SERVES : 4 - 6

- 6 artichokes (soak in salted water for 2 hours).
- 2 cups boiled and chopped chicken.
- 1 cup peeled and diced cucumber.
- 1 cup (150 ml.) classic mayonnaise (see page 84).
- 2 tbsps. finely chopped parsley or mint.
- 1 lettuce head.

- Prepare mayonnaise, cover and keep in cool place.
- Cook artichoke in boiling salted water for 20-25 minutes until tender enough to pull out the leaves easily. Drain and cool.
- Trim the bottom of the stem so they stand easily.
- Scoop out the centre of each artichoke leaving the outer 2 rows of leaves. Remove the hairy choke from the centre of each, so that the bottoms only are left.
- Mix together chicken, cucumber, finely chopped scooped out artichokes and mayonnaise.
- Fill the artichokes with the chicken mixture.
- Line a salad dish with lettuce. Place the artichokes on it, garnish with chopped parsley or mint.

Variation:

Cottage Cheese & Artichoke Salad:

Use 260 gms crumbled cottage cheese instead of chicken and use eggless mayonnaise (see page 84) and proceed as instructed above.

Facing Page:
Asparagus Soup (page 20)

JELLIED TOMATO AND EGG SALAD RING

PREPARATION TIME : 15 MINUTES   NO COOKING   SERVES : 4 - 6
CHILLING TIME : 2 HOURS

- 2 cups (300 ml.) cream of tomato soup.
- 1 cup thick yoghurt.
- ½ cup (75 ml.) green mayonnaise (see page 83).
- 1 small cucumber thinly sliced.
- 4 hard boiled eggs.
- 2 tbsps. gelatine.
- 2 level tsps. sugar.
- 2 level tsps. salt.
- ½ level tsp. pepper.
- 1 tsp. oil.
- a few lettuce leaves.
- 3-4 baby corns each cut into 4-5 pieces.
- 1 cup orange or sweet lime segments, pith & skin removed.

- Heat one cup soup and dissolve gelatine in it.
- Prepare lettuce leaves and keep them in refrigerator.
- Beat yoghurt lightly and keep aside.
- Chop two hard boiled eggs. Cut the remaining two eggs lengthwise into four pieces each.
- Combine in a bowl, mayonnaise, sugar salt, pepper, and gently stir in the 1 cup of tomato soup.
- Add beaten yoghurt and mix well.
- Stir in gelatine mixture and chopped eggs.
- Oil a ring mould. Cut cucumber slices in half. Arrange it around the ring mould and slowly pour the salad mixture into the mould.
- Allow it to set in the refrigerator for 2-3 hours.
- Unmould the salad just before serving.
- Break lettuce leaves into small pieces.
- Fill the centre with lettuce, baby corn and orange segments.

Vegetarian Jellied Tomato Salad Ring:
- Omit eggs. Use ¹/₂ cup grated Indian cottage cheese instead of chopped eggs.
- Use 1 cup shredded Indian cottage cheese instead of halved eggs and follow the remaining recipe as given above.
- Use eggless green mayonnaise instead of green mayonnaise.

Dieters tip: replace mayonnaise with orange dressing (see page 89).

Facing Page:

Thai Chicken Salad (page 52)
Salad Medley (page 50)

MOROCCAN TOMATO AND PEPPER SALAD

PREPARATION TIME : 30 MINUTES	COOKING TIME : 5 MINUTES	SERVES : 4 - 6

- 8 large tomatoes sliced.
- 6 red or green large Malwi chillies.
- 4 spring onions finely chopped.
- 3 tbsps. finely chopped parsley.
- ½ cup (75 ml.) Arabian salad dressing (see page 88).
- 1 level tsp. roasted ground cumin.
- ½ level tsp. sugar.
- 10 black olives sliced (optional).

- Grill the chillies until the skin blackens and cracks all over or put each on a fork or skewer and hold over an open gas flame. Allow to cool and peel. Remove stalk, pith and seeds and cut into strips.
- Mix Arabian dressing, cumin and sugar.
- Arrange some sliced tomatoes in a shallow salad bowl layer by layer, sprinkle the dressing, spring onions, cut chillies and top with tomato slices.
- Garnish with olives and parsley.

Non-Veg. Moroccan Salad with Chicken:
Add 2 cups boiled and chopped chicken at stage 3 and follow the recipe as given above.

SUNSHINE SLAW

PREPARATION TIME : 20 MINUTES, CHILLING TIME : 4 - 5 HOURS	NO COOKING	SERVES : 4 - 6

- 250 gms. white cabbage shredded washed and drained.
- 2 red apples.
- 250 gms. cheese (Vijaya or Amul).
- ⁴/₅ cup (120 ml.) lemon mayonnaise (see page 83).
- 1 level tbsp. mustard sauce.
- 1 level tsp. sugar.
- 2 tbsps. finely chopped fresh mint or parsley.
- juice of 1 lemon.

- Cut cheese into slivers and keep in the refrigerator.
- Core and dice apple with skin. Put in a bowl and sprinkle lemon juice.
- Mix mustard sauce and sugar with mayonnaise.
- In a bowl, combine cabbage, cheese, apple and parsley and pour enough dressing to coat well. Chill for 4-5 hours before serving.
- Serve remaining mayonnaise separately.

Vegetarian Sunshine Slaw:
Simply use eggless mayonnaise or white salad cream (see page 89) and proceed as given above.

RUSSIAN SALAD

PREPARATION TIME : 25 MINUTES | **COOKING TIME : 15 MINUTES** | **SERVES : 4 - 6**

- 2 cups new potatoes, diced and cooked.
- 1 cup carrots diced and cooked.
- ½ cup peas cooked.
- ½ cup french beans, chopped and cooked.
- 2 eggs boiled and chopped.
- 2 slices canned pineapple diced.
- 1 small lettuce.
- 1 cup classic mayonnaise (see page 84).
- 2 tbsps. yoghurt.
- ¼ level tsp. chilli powder.
- 1 sprig of mint.

- Prepare all the vegetables and chill.
- Mix together yoghurt, mayonnaise and chilli powder.
- Just before serving, mix together chilled vegetables, pineapple, eggs, half the dressing.
- Line a serving bowl with lettuce leaves and spoon the salad on top. Garnish with mint. Serve extra dressing separately.

Vegetarian Russian Salad:

Simply omit boiled eggs and use eggless mayonnaise. Follow the recipe as above.

CLASSIC COLESLAW

PREPARATION TIME : 20 MINUTES
CHILLING TIME: 4-5 HOURS | **NO COOKING** | **SERVES : 4 - 6**

- 250 gms. firm white cabbage trimmed and finely shredded.
- 1 large carrot scraped and grated.
- 1 large onion finely chopped.
- 1 stick celery trimmed and thinly sliced.
- 2 tbsps. finely chopped parsley.
- 1 level tsp. salt.
- ½ level tsp. dry mustard.
- ½ level tsp. ground pepper.
- ⁴/₅ cup (120 ml.) classic mayonnaise (see page 84).
- 2 sprigs of mint.

- Wash cabbage and drain well.
- Combine together in a large bowl, cabbage, carrot, parsley, onion, celery, salt, pepper and mustard. Mix well.
- Pour half the dressing over the vegetables and toss until well coated. Cover and chill in the refrigerator for 4 - 5 hours, before serving.
- Garnish with mint sprigs. Serve remaining mayonnaise separately.

Vegetarian Classic Coleslaw: Use eggless mayonnaise instead of classic mayonnaise and follow the recipe as above.

LOBSTER SALAD WITH MANGO DRESSING

| PREPARATION TIME : 30 MINUTES | COOKING TIME : 15 MINUTES | SERVES : 4 - 6 |

- 500 gms. lobster.
- 2 ripe mangoes, firm and chilled.
- 20 canned lychees.
- 2 tbsps. brown vinegar.
- 4-5 strands saffron.
- 2 red or green capsicums, deseeded and sliced.
- few lettuce leaves preferably assorted.
- 1 cup (150 ml.) mango mayonnaise (see page 85).

- Combine vinegar and saffron together and keep aside for 15 minutes.
- Select, wash and dry the lettuce leaves.
- Clean, trim and wash lobster and cook in boiling salted water. Remove the meat from the shell and slice them.
- Arrange lettuce leaves on one side of the serving dish. Place lobster slices beside the leaves. Sprinkle saffron mixture on the capsicum and lychees. Place them next to the lobster slices.
- Peel and cut mangoes into long strips and place mango strips in between the lobster slices.
- Pour some mango mayonnaise dressing on the other side of the lettuce leaves. Serve remaining dressing separately.

Vegetarian Chicken Salad with Mango Dressing:

Omit lobster, use vegetarian chicken (see page 76) or use boiled peeled and sliced taro sprinkled with salt and pepper instead and follow the remaining recipe as given above.

CHICKEN AND CORN SALAD

PREPARATION TIME : 30 MINUTES	CHILL FOR 1½ HOURS	SERVES : 4 - 6

- 1 kg. chicken cooked, deboned.
- 2 cups cooked corn kernels.
- 1 onion chopped.
- 1 small cucumber peeled and diced.
- ½ cup finely chopped mint.
- 1 cup (150 ml.) piquant mayonnaise (see page 83).
- few drops of tabasco or chilli oil (see page 82).
- 1 small lettuce shredded.
- 2 hard boiled eggs, sliced.
- 2 tomatoes sliced.

- Chop chicken meat. Mix together with corn kernels, onion, cucumber and mint. Chill until required.
- Make mayonnaise, cover and keep in refrigerator.
- Just before serving, pour half the mayonnaise over the chicken mixture and mix well.
- Line the salad bowl with shredded lettuce and spoon the salad on top.
- Sprinkle tabasco or chilli oil. Serve garnished with tomato slices and hard boiled eggs.

Vegetarian Cottage Cheese Corn Salad:
Omit chicken and eggs. Use 250 gms. shredded cottage cheese or toffu, braise slightly before adding to the salad. Eggless mayonnaise (see page 84) can be used instead of piquant mayonnaise; increase the tabasco a little and follow the recipe as given above.

SPICY TAI (THAI) SEAFOOD SALAD
(A SALAD RICH IN PROTEINS AND VITAMINS EXCELLENT FOR DIETERS)

PREPARATION TIME : 30 MINUTES **COOKING TIME : 5 MINUTES** **SERVES : 4 - 6**

- 500 gms. mussels.
- 10 large shrimps.
- 4 squids.
- 5 spring onions very thinly sliced.
- 1 cup crab meat.
- 5 tomatoes blanched and chopped roughly.
- 2 stalks lemon grass finely chopped.
- 1 cup finely chopped mint leaves.
- 2 onions sliced.
- 2 tsps. ground chilli paste.
- 2 level tsps. salt.
- 6 tomatoes.
- 2 tbsps. lemon or lime juice.
- 1 tbsp. fish sauce.
- 4 tbsps. piquant mayonnaise (see page 83).
- 1 small lettuce.

- If using fresh mussels, clean and cook in salted boiling water, until all mussels open. Strain and discard closed ones. Remove mussels from shells.
- Remove shell and devein shrimps. Cut each into two.
- Clean squid and cut into 2.5 cm. strips.
- Clean and break crab. Remove meat from shell. Cut into cubes.
- Combine shrimps, squid, crab meat in a sauce pan. Add salt and water.
- Cover and cook for 4-5 minutes. Remove and drain well.
- Prepare the lettuce leaves.
- Place mussels, shrimps, squid, crab meat in a large bowl. Add all the ingredients, toss well. Chill for 2 hours. Toss again before serving.
- Arrange lettuce on a serving dish and put salad in the centre.

Vegetarian Spicy Tai Salad:
- Omit shrimp, squid, crab and mussels.
- Use instead 1 cup thinly shredded Indian cottage cheese, 1 cup cooked soya nuggets chopped, 1 cup cooked taro chopped.
- Follow remaining recipe as given above.

SALAD NICOISE (FRANCE)

PREPARATION TIME : 20 MINUTES +
30 MINUTES CHILLING TIME

NO COOKING

SERVES : 4

- 250 gms. ripe and firm tomatoes.
- 1 small can tuna fish drained and flaked.
- 1 small cucumber peeled and sliced.
- 150 gms. french beans chopped and cooked.
- 2 cups French potato salad (see page 59).
- 10 black or green olives stoned.
- 3 hard boiled eggs shelled and quartered.
- 1 tbsp. chopped basil leaves.
- 2 tbsps. chopped fresh parsley.
- ½ cup (75 ml.) garlic French dressing (see page 88).
- 1 small lettuce.
- few canned, anchovies.

- Prepare the lettuce, line a salad bowl and keep in refrigerator.
- Halve tomatoes and anchovies and keep aside.
- Arrange potato salad and flaked tuna fish in the prepared salad bowl with the cucumber, beans, eggs, olives and tomatoes.
- Add parsley and basil to the French dressing. Mix well. Pour over the salad.
- Arrange anchovy fillets on top. Keep in refrigerator for 30 minutes before serving.
- Serve with French bread.

Vegetarian Salad Nicoise:

Omit fish and eggs. Use 1 cup bean sprouts and 1 cup crumbled Indian cottage cheese. Garnish with 4 tomato roses and follow the remaining recipe as instructed above.

SALAD MEDLEY

PREPARATION TIME : 20 MINUTES PLUS 2 HOURS CHILLING TIME	COOKING TIME : 25 MINUTES	SERVES : 4

- 2 beetroots.
- 6 medium potatoes.
- 1 large firm apple.
- 1 small celery stick chopped.
- 1 pickled gherkin chopped.
- 1 tbsp. finely chopped fresh parsley or mint.
- 1 tbsp. finely chopped fresh basil leaves.
- 1 cup piquant mayonnaise (see page 83).
- juice of one lime.

- Wash potatoes and beetroots and steam separately.
- Put both vegetables in cold water separately.
- Dice potatoes and beetroots and keep them in separate bowls.
- Core and dice apple, sprinkle lime juice over. Mix well and keep aside.
- Place all the vegetables and fruits in a large bowl and chill.
- Add the herbs and half the mayonnaise just before serving.
- Transfer the salad to a salad bowl. Serve remaining mayonnaise separately.

Vegetarian Salad Medley:
- Omit piquant mayonnaise. Use vegetarian piquant mayonnaise.
- Proceed as given above.

MIMOSA
(EGG AND ASPARAGUS SALAD)

PREPARATION TIME : 20 MINUTES	COOKING TIME : 15 MINUTES	SERVES : 8

- 500 gms. asparagus fresh or canned.
- 4 hard boiled eggs.
- ³/₅ cup (90 ml.) white salad cream (see page 89).
- ¹/₅ cup (30 ml.) double cream.
- 1 tbsp. tomato paste.
- 2 tbsps. sherry.
- 1 tsp. lemon juice.
- 1 level tsp. salt.
- ½ level tsp. pepper.
- ½ tsp. chilli powder.
- 2 tbsps. finely chopped parsley.

- If you are using canned asparagus, drain and wash.
- If you are using fresh asparagus, tie them in small bundles and soak them in boiling, salted water keeping them upright for 15 minutes and drain well. Open up the bundles and allow to cool.
- Chop asparagus and arrange in centre of four small individual salad dishes.
- Shell and cut each egg in half lengthways and arrange cut side down, on the asparagus and chill.
- Mix together white salad cream, tomato paste, sherry, lemon juice, double cream, salt and pepper.
- Cover the eggs with salad dressing just before serving.
- Sprinkle chilli powder and parsley on top.

Eggless Mimosa: Omit eggs. Use 250 gms. toffu or Indian cottage cheese cut into 1½" × 1½" squares. Make 8 squares. Place two squares on each dish over the chopped asparagus and cover with salad dressing.

TAI (THAI) CHICKEN SALAD
(EXCELLENT FOR SLIMMERS)

PREPARATION TIME : 30 MINUTES	COOKING TIME : 5 MINUTES	SERVES : 4 - 6

- 2 cups cooked chicken mince.
- 4 spring onions thinly sliced.
- 2 onions thinly sliced.
- 1 cup cashewnuts, fried.
- 8 dried red chillies, fried.
- $^1/_5$ cup (30 ml.) lime or lemon juice.
- 1 tsp. sugar.
- 1 tsp. grated rind of orange.
- 1 level tsp. salt.
- 1 medium cucumber thinly sliced.
- 4 tbsps. grated fresh ginger.
- 2 tbsps. finely chopped coriander leaves.
- 1 tsp. chilli powder.
- 1 tbsp. fish sauce (optional).
- $^2/_5$ cup (60 ml.) orange dressing (see page 89).
- lettuce leaves.

- Mix together in a small bowl orange dressing, fish sauce, chilli powder. Keep aside.
- Combine in a bowl, minced chicken with all the ingredients except fried chillies and cashewnuts.
- Prepare the lettuce leaves.
- Line a salad dish with lettuce leaves and arrange the chicken mixture on top. Chill before serving.
- Garnish with fried cashew nuts and chillies.

Vegetarian Tai Chicken Salad:
- Omit chicken and use 2 cups vegetarian chicken or cooked minced soya nuggets.

EGG AND CHEESE SALAD

PREPARATION TIME : 25 MINUTES +
1 HOUR CHILLING TIME.

NO COOKING

SERVES : 4

- 6 hard boiled eggs, shelled and quartered.
- 4 tomatoes blanched deseeded and quartered.
- 250 gms. cumin cottage cheese
- 2 medium onions.
- 1 tbsp. finely chopped fresh basil.
- 1 tsp. ground coriander seeds.
- 1 tsp. oregano.
- $^2/_5$ cup garlic French dressing (see page 88).
- 10 olives.

- Slice onions thinly and separate the rings.
- Thinly slice the cottage cheese 1" x 1" size.
- Mix ground coriander, oregano and chopped basil with French dressing.
- Place eggs, tomatoes, cheese, olives, $^3/_4$ of the onion rings in a bowl and pour over half the dressing. Toss gently. Chill before serving.
- Transfer salad to a glass salad bowl. Arrange remaining onion rings on top and sprinkle remaining French dressing.

Vegetarian Salad:

Omit eggs. Use 1 cup bean sprouts instead of eggs and proceed as above.

FATTOUSH

(LEBANESE BREAD SALAD. FATTOUSH MEANS MOISTENED BREAD, CHILLED, MIXED SALAD TOSSED WITH TOASTED BREAD CUBES).

PREPARATION TIME : 20 MINUTES | **COOKING TIME : 10 MINUTES** | **SERVES : 4 - 6**

- 2 khoubiz or naans.
- 2 medium cucumbers, peeled and diced.
- 2 large tomatoes cubed.
- 5 spring onions chopped.
- 2 capsicum diced.
- ½ cup chopped parsley.
- 2 tbsps. chopped mint.
- 2 green chillies deseeded and chopped.
- ¾ cup Arabian salad dressing (see page 88).
- 1 lettuce head, shredded.

- Cut the khoubiz or naan into squares. Grill them until golden brown.
- Place all the salad ingredients with herbs and bread pieces in a large bowl.
- Pour the dressing. Toss well and serve.

Note: Toasted bread cut into squares can be used instead of naan or khoubiz.

TABBOULEH
(LEBANESE BURGHUL AND PARSLEY SALAD)

PREPARATION TIME : 40 MINUTES + 1½ HOURS CHILLING TIME	NO COOKING	SERVES : 6

- 1 cup burghul (crushed wheat).
- 1½ cups finely chopped parsley.
- ½ cup finely chopped mint.
- ¾ cup finely chopped spring onions.
- 3 firm ripe tomatoes deseeded and finely chopped.
- 4 tbsps. lemon juice or lime juice.
- 1½ level tsps. salt.
- ½ level tsp. red chilli powder.
- ½ level tsp. black pepper.
- ⅖ cup (60 ml.) olive oil.
- 1 lettuce head.

- Wash and soak burghul in water for 40 minutes. Drain well through a sieve. Spread onto a cloth and leave to dry.
- Clean and wash parsley. Remove thick stalks. Wrap in a tea towel and place in refrigerator until required.
- Put burghul and spring onions in a bowl and mix thoroughly.
- Mix together olive oil, salt, pepper, chilli powder and lemon juice.
- Chop parsley and add to the burghul mixture.
- Stir in lemon juice and olive oil mixture. Toss well.
- Add chopped tomatoes and mint. Mix well (You may remove the skin of tomatoes if desired before adding to the salad).
- Cover and chill for 1½ hours before serving.
- Serve in a salad bowl lined with crisp lettuce leaves and place burghul mixture in the centre.
- Serve extra lemon juice mixed with salt separately.

CURRIED RICE AND CHICKEN SALAD

| PREPARATION TIME : 20 MINUTES + CHILLING TIME: 1 - 2 HRS. | COOKING TIME : 10 MINUTES | SERVES : 4 - 6 |

- ½ cup basmati rice.
- 1 cup cooked and chopped chicken or any meat.
- 2 large slices canned pineapple rings.
- 50 gms. cheese.
- 1 tbsp. grated orange rind.
- 1 cup orange segments, pith removed.
- ⁴/₅ cup (120 ml.) curried mayonnaise (see page 86).
- 1 level tsp. chilli powder, (optional).
- ½ level tsp. pepper.
- 1 small lettuce head.
- 2 tbsps. finely chopped mint or parsley.
- 1 tsp. salt.

- Cook rice for 10 minutes in boiling salted water until tender, but not mushy. Rinse with cold water and drain well and chill.
- Just before serving, combine in a bowl chicken, rice, half the mayonnaise, orange rind and toss well.
- Place pineapple slices on a kitchen towel and pat dry. Chop pineapple and add to the rice mixture.
- Sprinkle chilli powder and pepper. Toss well.
- Cut cheese into thin strips. Add cheese and orange segments carefully to the rice mixture. Lightly toss. Add more mayonnaise if needed.
- Line a salad dish with lettuce and arrange rice salad on it. Garnish with mint or parsley.
- Serve remaining mayonnaise separately.

Vegetarian Rice Salad:

- Use 250 gms. cooked and prepared soyabean nuggets instead of chicken. Wash thoroughly. Drain well. Shred them and sprinkle 4 tablespoons sherry or cooking wine.
- Use vegetarian curry mayonnaise instead of curry mayonnaise and proceed as above.

MEXICAN CHICKEN AND BEAN SALAD
(WITH HOT MEXICAN DRESSING AND VEGETARIAN MEXICAN SALAD)

PREPARATION TIME : 20 MINUTES — SERVES : 4 - 6

- 1.25 kg. chicken, boiled.
- 2 cups cooked red kidney beans.
- 1 stick celery chopped.
- 25 gms. gherkins sliced.
- 3 hard boiled eggs sliced.
- 1 medium onion chopped.
- 1 small lettuce head.
- 2 tbsps. finely chopped parsley or mint.
- 1 cup (150 ml.) hot Mexican dressing (see page 87).

- Drain well cooked kidney beans. Chill.
- Remove meat from chicken, chop roughly and chill.
- Place chicken, beans, celery, onion and gherkins in a bowl. Add half of the dressing. Mix well.
- Line a shallow salad bowl with lettuce leaves and place chicken and bean mixture on it.
- Arrange egg slices on one side of the dish just before serving.
- Serve extra dressing separately.
- Garnish with chopped parsley.

Vegetarian Mexican Salad:
Omit chicken and eggs. Use 2 cups cooked soya nuggets instead of chicken and use 50 gms. cottage cheese instead of eggs. Slice them thinly and arrange on one side of dish, sprinkle finely chopped mint on top.

OR
Omit eggs and chicken. Add 250 gms. shredded cottage cheese or toffu and 1 cup bean sprouts.

MOULDED CHICKEN SALAD

| PREPARATION TIME : 1 HR. + 2 HOURS CHILLING TIME | COOKING TIME : 15 - 20 MINUTES   SERVES : 4 - 6 |

- 2 cups cooked and finely diced chicken.
- 1 small cucumber peeled and finely diced.
- 1 small onion finely chopped.
- 1 small carrot scraped and finely sliced.
- 1 large tomato deseeded and finely sliced.
- 2 tbsps. finely chopped parsley.
- 1½ cups chicken stock (see page 79).
- 2 tsps. gelatine.
- 1 tsp. salt.
- ½ tsp. pepper.
- lettuce leaves.
- ½ tsp. salad oil.

- Put chicken, onion and carrot in a large sauce pan with stock. Heat it for 15 minutes. Let it stand for 1 hour.
- Drain the stock in another vessel and heat again. Dissolve gelatine in ½ cup stock and allow it to cool.
- Lightly oil a salad mould with ½ teaspoon salad oil.
- Mix chicken, onion, carrot, salt and pepper with remaining stock.
- Add gelatine mixture. Keep 2 tablespoons aside.
- Cover the bottom of the mould with 2 tablespoons gelatine and sprinkle chopped tomato. Spoon salad mixture into the mould.
- Chill in refrigerator for 2 hours. Line a salad dish with lettuce leaves and turn out the mould on it and arrange cucumber slices around it and sprinkle chopped parsley on top.

Moulded Mock Meat Salad:

Use 250 gms. boiled and roughly chopped soya nuggets instead of chicken, and replace chicken stock with vegetable stock and proceed as above.

Facing Page:

Cherry Soup (page 12)

Moulded Chicken Salad (page 58)

FRENCH POTATO SALAD

PREPARATION TIME : 30 MINUTES | **COOKING TIME : 15 MINUTES** | **SERVES : 4**

- 500 gms. potatoes.
- 2 spring onions sliced thinly with little green tops.
- 3 tbsps. white vinegar preferably white wine vinegar (see page 82).
- 2 level tsps. salt.
- 3 level tsps. dry mustard.
- ½ cup finely chopped fresh parsley.
- ²/₅ cup (60 ml.) chicken stock or white stock (see page 79).
- 4 tbsps. olive oil or salad oil.
- water.
- 1 small lettuce.

- Boil water in a large sauce pan with 1 teaspoon salt.
- Cook potatoes in boiling salted water for 10-15 minutes until done but firm. Do not over-cook. Remove and drain them thoroughly in a sieve.
- Peel and slice potatoes, place them in a bowl.
- Heat chicken stock and pour it over the warm potatoes. Toss and allow it to stand for 20 minutes until the stock is completely absorbed.
- Put in a small bowl salt, mustard and vinegar. Mix well, add to the potatoes and toss gently. Keep aside for 10 minutes.
- Sprinkle oil, spring onions, parsley; coat them well.
- Prepare the lettuce. Line the salad bowl with lettuce leaves. Place potato slices in the centre.
- Chill before serving. Put a sprig of parsley in the centre.

Potato salad with chicken:

Use 500 gms. whole small new potatoes instead of sliced ones and 2 cups cooked and diced chicken. Toss well with dressing and herbs and follow recipe as given above.

Note: Chopped salami or luncheon meat cut into cubes can also be used instead of chicken.

Facing Page:

Spaghetti, Chicken and Pineapple Salad (page 61)
Almond Soup (page 26)
Cherry Soup (page 12)
Moulded Chicken Salad (page 58)
Thai Chicken Salad (page 52)
Salad Medley (page 50)

LAMB SALAD MOUSSE

PREPARATION TIME : 30 MINUTES	CHILLING TIME : 2 HOURS	SERVES : 4 - 6

- 2 cups lamb or chicken cooked and minced.
- 1 cup (150 ml.) classic mayonnaise (see page 84).
- ½ cup (75 ml.) double cream.
- 1 onion grated.
- 3 tbsps. sweet pickle finely minced.
- 2 tbsps. finely chopped parsley.
- 1 level tsp. salt.
- 3 egg whites beaten.
- 2 tbsps. gelatine.
- 1½ cups hot water.
- ½ cup cold water.
- 1 tbsp. worcestershire sauce.
- 1 tsp. tabasco (optional).
- ½ cup (75 ml.) French dressing (see page 88).
- 1 level tsp. chilli powder (optional).
- a few lettuce leaves.

- Grind minced lamb or chicken until smooth.
- Beat cream lightly.
- Dissolve gelatine in a little cold water, then add hot water and mix well.
- Mix together ground chicken, onion, parsley, pickle, chilli powder, salt, worcestershire sauce, tabasco, mayonnaise and cream thoroughly.
- Stir in gelatine. Mix well.
- Fold in beaten egg whites gently. Mix and pour into a lightly greased salad mould and chill until firm.
- Line a salad dish with lettuce and unmould on it. Serve with French dressing.

Vegetarian Salad Mousse:
Omit chicken or lamb and egg whites.
Use 250 gms. boiled soya nuggets, and 100 gms. cottage cheese instead and grind them until smooth.

SPAGHETTI, CHICKEN AND PINEAPPLE SALAD

PREPARATION TIME : 20 MINUTES | **COOKING TIME : 10 MINUTES** | **SERVES : 6**

- 2 cups spaghetti or shell pasta.
- 2 cups cooked and diced chicken.
- 2 slices pineapple (canned) diced.
- 1 cup cooked red kidney beans.
- 2 green chillies deseeded and chopped.
- 1 small onion finely chopped.
- $^4/_5$ cups (120 ml.) lemon mayonnaise (see page 83).
- 1 tbsp. finely chopped fresh mint.
- 1 level tsp. salt.
- ½ level tsp. pepper.
- few lettuce leaves.

- Soak red kidney beans overnight and cook in salted water until soft. Drain well and keep aside.
- Cook the pasta in boiling salted water for 10 minutes until tender. Drain well. Immediately rinse in cold water and drain again.
- Combine together in a bowl spaghetti, chicken, beans, onion, chillies.
- Pat dry the diced pineapple on a kitchen towel or paper and add it to the salad.
- Sprinkle salt and pepper. Chill until required.
- Prepare lettuce leaves, break them roughly.
- Pour half the mayonnaise on to the salad mixture just before serving. Toss well.
- Line a salad bowl with lettuce leaves and arrange the salad on it. Serve remaining mayonnaise separately. Sprinkle chopped mint on top.

Vegetarian Spaghetti Salad:
Simply omit chicken and proceed as above or you may use 1 cup mashed cottage cheese instead of chicken.

SALMAGUNDY

PREPARATION TIME : 25 MINUTES

COOKING TIME : 8 MINUTES

- 250 gms. roasted duck meat.
- 250 gms. roasted chicken.
- 4 large carrots, peeled.
- 4 medium potatoes boiled, peeled and diced.
- 2 sticks celery trimmed and thinly sliced.
- 2 large firm tomatoes skinned and sliced.
- 1½ cups cooked green peas.
- 2 medium cucumbers thinly sliced.
- 1 cup (150 ml.) basic French dressing (see page 88).
- 3 hard boiled eggs.
- few radish, sliced thinly.
- 4 gherkins cut into fans.
- few sprigs of parsley to garnish.

- Cut duck and chicken meat into ¼" wide and 1½" long strips, put them in a bowl and sprinkle French dressing and toss well.
- Cut carrots into ¼" wide and 2½" long strips. Cook in boiling salted water for 8 minutes. Drain and sprinkle little French dressing. Toss well.
- Sprinkle dressing lightly on diced potatoes and sliced cucumber, celery and radish.
- Take a large oval salad platter for layering the Salmagundy. Place diced potatoes at the bottom of the plate to give a flat base.
- Arrange chicken and duck meat strips alternately around the diced potatoes.
- Remember to make each layer inside the one below so that the lower layers may also be seen.
- Arrange the outer layer with cucumber slightly inside the carrot layer so that the carrot sticks can be seen.
- Put gently boiled peas in the centre and arrange radish slices around it.
- Place tomato slices on top of the peas.
- Arrange celery slices on top of tomato slices.
- Put gherkin fans at four sides of the salad plate.
- Halve the boiled eggs. Top each half with little mayonnaise, garnish with radish slice and parsley. Now arrange them alternately with the gherkin fans around the edges of the dish.

Vegetarian Salmagundy:

Omit eggs, chicken and duck pieces. Replace with shredded cottage cheese and strips of Amul cheese, sprinkled with dressing.

Note: Preparing Salmagundy is the best way to use left over roasted duck and chicken the next day. Traditionally Salmagundy is made for grand dinner parties and the finished dish can be as high as 2 feet. Small pieces of fish, vegetables and other salad ingredients are also used.

WALDORF SALAD

PREPARATION TIME : 20 MINUTES	CHILLING TIME : 1 - 2 HOURS	SERVES : 4

- 4 large firm red apples.
- 1 cup shelled walnuts.
- 2 sticks celery trimmed and sliced.
- 1 tsp. sugar.
- 4 tbsps. lime or lemon juice.
- ³/₅ cup (90 ml.) lemon mayonnaise (see page 83).
- 1 small lettuce head.

- Chop walnuts (keeping a few whole for garnishing).
- Core the apples and dice three apples. Slice one apple and keep separate. Sprinkle lemon juice and sugar on diced apples. Keep them aside.
- Put diced apples in a bowl. Add 1 tablespoon of mayonnaise and toss well, chill.
- Just before serving add the sliced celery and the chopped walnuts to the diced apple mixture.
- Add the remaining mayonnaise. Toss well.
- Serve in a bowl, lined with lettuce leaves and garnish with apple slices and whole walnuts.

Vegetarian Waldorf Salad:
Use 1 recipe vegetarian lemon mayonnaise (see page 83) instead of lemon mayonnaise.

PEACH SALAD WITH RED WINE

PREPARATION TIME : 20 MINUTES AND CHILLING TIME : 2 HOURS	NO COOKING	SERVES : 4-6

- 500 gms. ripe firm large peaches.
- 4 tbsps. lemon juice.
- 1 tbsp. castor sugar.
- 1 cup red wine.
- 1 tsp. grated rind of lemon.
- 1 tsp. finely chopped fresh basil (optional).

- Wash and dry peaches. Peel and slice, discard the stone.
- Sprinkle sugar, lemon juice, grated rind and toss well.
- Pour wine and mix well. Chill.
- Transfer into a glass bowl and serve garnished with basil.

AVOCADO, MUSHROOM AND SUNFLOWER SALAD

| PREPARATION TIME : 15 MINUTES | COOKING TIME : 10 MINUTES | SERVES : 4 - 6 |

- 250 gms. mushrooms cleaned and sliced.
- 4 stalks of celery thinly sliced.
- 8 stuffed olives (bottled) sliced.
- 2 avocados, peeled, halved and stoned and cut into 4-6 pieces.
- 4 tbsps. lemon juice.
- 1 tbsp. sunflower seeds.
- 1 tsp. dried thyme.
- $^2/_5$ cup (60 ml.) Arabian salad dressing (see page 88).
- 1 tbsp. finely chopped parsley.
- 1 small lettuce.

- Combine all the ingredients in a bowl.
- Add 2 tablespoons dressing. Toss well and chill.
- Just before serving add remaining dressing and toss well.
- Prepare lettuce, arrange on a salad dish and pile the salad in the centre. Garnish with chopped parsley.

Note: Cook mushroom for a few minutes in boiling salted water if using fresh mushrooms. If canned mushroom is used, wash well before cutting.

BROCCOLI AND COTTAGE CHEESE SALAD

(EXCELLENT SALAD FOR DIETERS)

PREPARATION TIME : 20 MINUTES	COOKING TIME : 15 MINUTES	SERVES : 4

- 1 small broccoli broken into florets.
- 250 gms. chilli cottage cheese.
- 1 cup cooked and chopped shrimps.
- 1 large onion, sliced and rings removed.
- 2 tbsps. lemon juice.
- ½ cup pomegranate.
- 1 tbsp. finely chopped mint.
- ½ cup (75 ml.) mustard dressing (see page 90).
- 1 tsp. salt.

- Cook Broccoli florets in boiling salted water until just tender. Drain and wash in cold water. Again drain well. Leave it to cool.
- Slice cottage cheese into 1" x 1" thin slices.
- Put together in a bowl broccoli, shrimps, cottage cheese, pomegranate and lemon juice. Mix well. Chill until required.
- Just before serving pour half the dressing over the salad. Toss well.
- Transfer into a salad bowl. Arrange the onion rings on top. Sprinkle chopped mint and serve remaining dressing separately.

Vegetarian Broccoli Salad:

Omit shrimps and follow the remaining recipe as above.

CAULIFLOWER SALAD WITH ORANGE DRESSING

PREPARATION TIME : 20 MINUTES PLUS 1 HOUR CHILLING TIME	NO COOKING	SERVES : 4

- 500 gms. cauliflower trimmed.
- 1 onion sliced and rings separated.
- 1 clove garlic crushed.
- ½ cup (75 ml.) orange dressing (see page 89).
- 1 tsp. grated orange rind.
- 1 tsp. tabasco sauce.
- 1 tsp. salt.
- 1 small lettuce, wash the lettuce and keep in cool place.

- Break the cauliflower into small florets about 1 inch size. Soak them in boiling salted water for 20 minutes. Drain and wash in cold water again. Drain well.
- Put cauliflower florets in a bowl together with onion rings and orange rind and half the dressing. Toss well and chill.
- Rub crushed garlic in a salad bowl and remove the garlic. Line it with lettuce leaves. Place cauliflower in the centre and sprinkle tabasco on top.

Note: You may also garnish with orange slices cut with peel and then cut each slice into half. Arrange them around the salad. If you garnish with orange slices, use a salad dish instead of a bowl.

LETTUCE & TOMATO SALAD

(AN EVERY DAY SALAD FROM MEGHALAYA)

PREPARATION TIME : 15 MINUTES	NO COOKING	SERVES : 4

- 1 small lettuce.
- 6 ripe firm tomatoes, sliced.
- 2 tbsps. garlic vinegar (see page 86).
- 2 tbsps. olive or corn oil.
- 1 tsp. salt.
- ½ tsp. pepper.
- 1 tsp. sugar.

- Remove outer leaves of lettuce, wash and dry lettuce leaves. Break them into large pieces.
- Place them in a bowl, add sliced tomatoes.
- Mix all remaining ingredients together and pour over lettuce and tomatoes. Toss well. Chill.
- Toss again before serving.

SIMPLE POTATO SALAD WITH ORANGE MAYONNAISE
(EXCELLENT FOR CHILDREN)

PREPARATION TIME : 5 MINUTES, CHILLING TIME : 2 HOURS	COOKING TIME : 15 MINUTES SERVES : 4 - 6

- 500 gms. medium size potatoes washed.
- 1 onion finely chopped.
- 1 cup (150 ml.) orange mayonnaise (see page 85).
- 2 tbsps. finely chopped mint or parsley.
- 2 tsps. salt.

- Boil water in a large saucepan with 1 teaspoon salt. Cook potatoes until tender, not over soft.
- Remove from water and leave aside until cool enough to handle, but not cold.
- Cut potatoes into neat cubes. Place them in a large bowl.
- Add mayonnaise, onion and parsley. Toss well and chill.

Vegetarian Potato Salad:
Omit orange mayonnaise. Use vegetarian orange mayonnaise instead.

Dieters' tip:
Omit mayonnaise, use orange dressing instead.

CHICKEN AND MELON SALAD WITH GINGER

PREPARATION TIME : 15 MINUTES | **COOKING TIME : 1½ HOURS** | **SERVES : 4**

- 1 medium sized honeydew melon (sakkarbatti).
- 1½ kg. chicken, skin removed.
- 3 cups cooking red wine.
- 1 carrot peeled and sliced.
- 1 bay leaf.
- 1 medium onion sliced.
- 1 cinnamon stick.
- 1 tsp. salt.
- 8 peppercorns.
- ⁴/₅ cup (120 ml.) French dressing (see page 88).
- 1 medium onion finely chopped.
- 1 small celery trimmed and sliced.
- ½ level tsp. dry ground ginger.
- ½ level tsp. chilli powder.
- 25 gms. fresh ginger finely grated.
- 4 tbsps. lime or lemon juice.
- 1 green chilli deseeded and finely chopped.
- ½ cup (75 ml.) cream. } mix together
- 2 tbsps. plain yoghurt }
- ⁴/₅ cup (120 ml.) lemon mayonnaise (see page 83).
- 2 tbsps. finely chopped mint or parsley.
- 1 tbsp. vegetable oil.

One day before:
- Put salt, wine, carrot, onion, cinnamon, peppercorns, and bay leaf in a large sauce pan with chicken. Bring to the boil. Lower heat and simmer for 1½ hours until chicken is tender, add water, if needed. Leave chicken to cool in wine.
- When cold, remove the chicken meat and shred finely. Put in a bowl and pour French dressing over it. Mix well and leave to marinate overnight in the refrigerator.

Next day:
- Heat oil in a fry pan. Saute onion, dry ginger for 2-3 minutes. Remove and allow it to cool.
- Put the melon in the refrigerator. Place onion mixture in a bowl, add grated ginger, celery, yoghurt, cream mixture, chilli powder, chopped chilli and half the mayonnaise. Mix well. All ingredients should be well coated. Chill.
- Halve the melon into two. Scoop out all the flesh and chop roughly. Add lemon juice and mix.
- Combine all ingredients in a large bowl, add more mayonnaise if needed. Toss gently. Chill for 15-20 minutes.
- Pile the salad into the melon shell. Garnish with chopped parsley. Serve remaining mayonnaise separately.

Dieters' tip:
- Use piquant French dressing instead of mayonnaise.

Vegetarian Chicken and Melon Salad:
- Use vegetarian chicken (page 76) or shredded cottage cheese and follow the recipe as above.

CUCUMBER, BEAN SPROUTS AND FISH SALAD

PREPARATION TIME : 25 MINUTES	COOKING TIME : 15 MINUTES SERVES : 4 - 6
CHILLING TIME : 2 HOURS	

- 1 large pomfret or 500 gms. any white fish.
- 1½ cups mung bean sprouts, cleaned and washed.
- 2 tbsps. lime or lemon juice.
- 1 tsp. grated rind of lime.
- 1 cup (150 ml.) 1000 Island dressing (see page 90).
- 1 medium cucumber peeled, deseeded and diced.
- 2 level tsps. salt.

For garnishing:
- few cooked, peeled prawns.
- 2 lemons cut into wedges.
- few mint leaves or parsley.

- Cook fish in boiling salted water until done. Drain, remove skin and flake fish coarsely in a bowl and discard bones.
- Sprinkle lemon juice thoroughly over the flaked fish.
- Combine in a bowl fish, cucumber, bean sprouts, lemon rind, chopped mint or parsley.
- Add half of the dressing and toss well. Chill.
- Just before serving, add remaining dressing and mix well.
- Pile the mixture into individual salad dishes and garnish with lemon wedges, a sprig of mint and place one prawn in each dish.
- Or serve in a large salad bowl and garnish with prawns, mint and lemon wedges.

Vegetarian Cucumber, Bean Sprouts and Fish Salad:
- Use 2 cups thinly sliced 2" × 2" square Indian cottage cheese instead of fish or equal amount of cooked peeled, flaked taro and follow remaining recipe as instructed.
- Use vegetarian 1000 Island dressing.

Dieters' tip:
- Omit mayonnaise. Use Italian dressing (see page 87) or hot Mexican dressing (see page 87).

APPLE BANANA AND RAISIN SLAW

PREPARATION TIME : 20 MINUTES AND CHILLING TIME : 2 HOURS	NO COOKING	SERVES : 4 - 6

- 2 cups finely shredded white cabbage. (use inner part).
- 2 small bananas.
- 2 firm Kashmiri or Simla apples.
- 2 tbsps. seedless raisins, washed and dried.
- 1 stick celery thinly sliced.
- 6 dates stoned and chopped.
- 3 tbsps. crushed, roasted peanuts for garnishing.
- 1 tsp. roasted caraway seeds.
- ½ cup (75 ml.) lime or lemon juice.
- ½ cup lemon mayonnaise. (see page 83).
- 1 tsp. salt.
- ½ level tsp. pepper.
- 2 tbsps. cream.
- 1 tsp. vinegar.

- Core and dice apples. Sprinkle half the lemon juice.
- Peel and slice bananas.
- Mix together mayonnaise, cream, vinegar, salt and pepper.
- Combine in a bowl cabbage, apples, bananas, dates, raisins, caraway seeds, celery. Gently spoon dressing on the salad and toss well until the ingredients are thoroughly coated. Chill.
- Just before serving, toss again. Add more dressing if needed or serve separately.
- Garnish with roasted peanuts.

Vegetarian Apple, Banana, Raisin Salad:
Use vegetarian lemon mayonnaise instead and proceed as above.

Dieters' tip:
Omit mayonnaise, cream and vinegar. Add garlic French dressing instead.

TUNA FISH AND CHEESE SALAD WITH MUSTARD DRESSING

PREPARATION TIME : 15 MINUTES
AND CHILLING TIME : 1½ HRS

NO COOKING   SERVES : 4

- 1 cup canned tuna fish flaked.
- 1 cup crumbled jeera cottage cheese.
- 1 cup finely chopped canned pineapple.
- few extra pineapple slices cut into half.
- 1 level tsp. salt.
- ½ level tsp. pepper.
- ³/₅ cup (90 ml.) mustard dressing (see page 90).
- lettuce leaves.

- Combine in a bowl, tuna fish, cheese, pineapple, salt, pepper and half the dressing. Toss well and chill.
- Just before serving toss the salad again and spoon more dressing. Mix well.
- Line the salad dish with lettuce. Pile the salad in the centre and arrange pineapple slices around.

Vegetarian Tuna and Cheese Salad:
- Omit tuna fish. Add 1 cup diced apple instead and proceed as given above.

APRICOT COTTAGE CHEESE AND GINGER SALAD

PREPARATION TIME : 20 MINUTES
AND CHILLING TIME : 1½ HOURS

NO COOKING   SERVES : 4 - 6

- 500 gms. apricots stoned and halved.
- 1 cup crumbled Indian cottage cheese.
- 1 cup shelled and roughly crushed walnuts.
- 1 cup grapes.
- 1 tbsps. grated fresh ginger.
- 1 level tsp. castor sugar.
- 1 tbsp. finely chopped mint.
- 2 tbsps. lemon juice.
- ³/₅ cup (90 ml.) orange dressing (see page 89).
- 1 small lettuce.

- Put cottage cheese in a bowl. Add 2 tablespoons dressing. Coat well.
- Wash, dry and cut grapes into two if large.
- Combine the cottage cheese, apricots, walnuts, grapes, castor sugar, ginger and lemon juice. Toss well and chill.
- Just before serving, add remaining dressing and toss well.
- Prepare lettuce and line the salad dish with it. Arrange the salad in the centre and sprinkle chopped mint on top.

ACCOMPANIMENTS FLAVOURED BUTTER
TO SERVE WITH SOUP

Hot and crusty French bread and rolls makes a pleasant alternative to toast and go well with most of the soups, but melba toast, cheese straws, white and brown bread slices can also be served for a change. You can use different flavoured butter for breads. These also can be made at home.

Cheese and Mustard Butter:

Mix 3 teaspoons of mustard powder, 2 tablespoons grated cheese, 1 tablespoon finely chopped parsley with ½ cup softened butter.

Mint Butter:

Mix 3 tablespoons freshly chopped mint and 1 teaspoon lemon juice, 1 teaspoon grated lemon rind with ½ cup softened butter.

Curried Butter:

Mix 2 teaspoons of curry powder, ½ teaspoon garam masala with ½ cup softened butter.

Spicy Butter:

Mix 1 teaspoon chilli powder, 1 tablespoon finely chopped coriander leaves with ½ cup softened butter.

Garlic Butter: See garlic bread (page 74)

Serve each of them put in individual bowls. Soup accompaniments are mostly served with hot soups.

BREAD STICKS

PREPARATION TIME : 2½ HOURS	COOKING TIME : 15 MINUTES	SERVES : 6-8

- 4 cups flour.
- 1 tsp. sugar.
- 1 tsp. salt.
- 2 tsps. dry yeast.
- 1 tbsp. margarine.
- 2 cups (300 ml.) lukewarm water.
- milk for glazing.
- 2 tbsps. poppy seeds or sesame seeds.

- Sieve salt and flour in a bowl.
- Sprinkle yeast and sugar in the water, stir until they dissolve and leave until frothy.
- Mix margarine with flour. Pour in yeast mixture and mix to a soft dough.
- Place the dough on a light floured flat surface and knead until smooth.
- Place the dough in a lightly oiled plastic bag and leave in a warm place for 1 hour to rise until double in size.
- Turn out the dough on a clean flat surface and knead again until smooth. Return to the oiled plastic bag and allow it to rise again.
- Turn it out again onto a lightly floured flat surface and knead lightly.
- Divide the dough into small balls the size of a walnut and roll each into a strand about 8" - 9" long. Place them on a lightly greased and floured baking tray.
- Brush with milk. Sprinkle with poppy seeds or sesame seeds. Cover with a muslin cloth and allow to rise for 20 minutes, in a warm place.
- Bake in a preheated hot oven 220°C - 425°F – gas mark 7 for 15 minutes until golden brown and crisp.
- Cool on a rack and store in an airtight container.

SIMPLE DINNER ROLL

PREPARATION TIME : 1 HR. 45 MINS.

COOKING TIME : 10-15 MINS • MAKES : 8-10 ROLLS

- 1 recipe French bread dough (see page 78).
- 2 tbsps. white sesame seeds.
- milk to glaze.

- Make the dough as instructed. Divide into 8 - 10 parts and place them on a flat surface.
- Flatten each piece with your palm, then rotate the hand using firm pressure at first, then, gently ease of the pressure and put the round between both your palms and gently form a roll.
- Place them on a lightly greased and floured baking tray and leave to rise in a warm place for 35 minutes.
- Brush the tops with milk and sprinkle sesame seeds.
- Bake in a preheated hot oven (230°C - 450°F – gas mark 8) for 10 - 15 minutes.

GARLIC BREAD

PREPARATION TIME : 20 MINUTES

COOKING TIME : 20 MINUTES   **SERVES : 4**

- 1 French bread freshly baked.
- 100 gms. butter, softened.
- 10 cloves garlic ground to a paste.
- 2 tbsps. finely chopped mint or parsley.
- 1 level tsp. freshly ground black pepper.
- 1 tsp. chilli powder (optional).
- foil.

- Mix together softened butter, garlic, mint, chilli powder and pepper. Beat well.
- Slice the French bread diagonally but not right through (base should be intact).
- Spread garlic butter over both sides of each slice and wrap the loaf in foil.
- Bake in a preheated hot oven 220°C-425°F – gas mark 7 for 15-20 minutes.
- Open up the foil for the last two minutes for a crisp crust. Serve warm with soups and salad.

FOCACCIA ALL'OLIO CON CIPOLLE
(SIMPLE ITALIAN BREAD WITH ONION)

PREPARATION TIME : 15 MINUTES	COOKING TIME : 20 MINUTES	SERVES : 6

- 500 gms. wheat or plain flour.
- 30 gms. fresh yeast.
- 2 level tsps. salt.
- 1 cup lukewarm water.
- 8 large onions thinly sliced.
- 1¼ cups/190 ml. olive oil.

(if using dry yeast, then sprinkle over ½ cup hot milk before using; also can be made with 3 level tsps. baking powder added to the flour).

- Mix yeast and water, add to the flour. Add enough water to make a soft dough.
- Oil a flat 11" × 9" × 2" baking tray. Spread the dough and press lightly. Spoon oil on top, sprinkle salt.
- Arrange onion slices to cover the top. Spoon oil again thoroughly.
- Bake in a hot oven 220°C - 450°F – gas mark 7 for 20 minutes. Remove and cool.
- Cut into 4" × 2" pieces before serving.

VEGETARIAN FISH OR MOCK FISH

PREPARATION TIME : 10 MINUTES	COOKING TIME : 45 MINUTES

- 1 pkt. ready made idli mix.
- 1 cup fine bread crumbs.
- 1 cup milk.
- Oil for deep frying.

- Prepare the mixture as directed on the packet.
- Oil lightly a square cake tin. Pour in the mixture and steam.
- Cut the steamed rice cake into rectangles. Should resemble fish fillets.
- Sprinkle milk lightly over the cut rectangles. Coat well with bread crumbs.
- Heat oil and deep fry the rectangle pieces a few at a time. Drain well.
- Use as required.

VEGETARIAN CHICKEN

PREPARATION TIME : 20 MINUTES	COOKING TIME : 20 MINUTES

- 12 pieces soya bean milk skins.
- $^2/_3$ tsp. gourmet powder.
- 1 tsp. salt.
- 4 tbsps. cooking wine.
- 6 tbsps. sesame oil.
- $^1/_2$ cup water.

- In a bowl mix cooking wine, salt, gourmet powder and make a seasoning sauce.
- Soak bean milk skins thoroughly in this sauce. Remove and spread out on a work board. Cut off uneven ends. Make into a rectangular piece.
- Sprinkle sesame oil. Arrange them one overlapping another and roll them into a cylinder. Press it into a flat roll of about $1^1/_2$ inches wide.
- Grease the inside of a deep dish with oil and arrange the roll in it. Cover it with another dish, a size smaller.
- Steam over boiling water for 20 minutes. Remove and cool, brush with sesame oil to prevent drying. Leave it in the same plate.
- Cut into pieces as required.

Note: While making the roll use cut off edges also while rolling. The roll should not be made overnight. Weight on top while steaming should not be heavy. Remove the weight and cover only after steamed roll has become cool.

CROUTONS

	COOKING TIME : 15 MINUTES

- A few slices of stale bread.
- oil for frying.

- Dice the slices into small squares.
- Heat oil in a small fry pan, fry bread until golden brown.
- Use for garnishing soups and salads.

WHOLE WHEAT SCONES

PREPARATION TIME : 20 MINUTES MAKES : 8	COOKING TIME : 15 MINUTES	SERVES : 4

- 2 cups whole wheat flour.
- 50 gms. margarine.
- ½ cup (75 ml.) yoghurt.
- 1 level tsp. soda-bi-carb.
- ½ level tsp. salt.

- Sieve flour and salt together. Add margarine, mix it with a fork or fingers until the mixture resembles breadcrumbs.
- Mix together yoghurt and soda-bi-carb. Leave aside for 3 - 4 minutes until frothy.
- Stir the yoghurt mixture into the flour. Knead well, make a soft and smooth dough.
- Roll out the dough on a lightly floured board to a thickness of 1 cm.
- Cut out scones using a 5 cm (2") fluted biscuit cutter.
- Place scones on a lightly greased and floured baking tray.
- Bake in a preheated hot oven 220°C - 425°F — gas mark 7 for 15 minutes until done. Cool and serve.

MELBA TOAST

	COOKING TIME : 20 MINUTES

- A few thin slices of stale bread (this is an excellent way to use up a day old bread).

- Remove the crust from the slices.
- Cut them into triangles.
- Arrange on a baking tray, bake in moderately hot oven 350°F - 180°C, gas mark 4, until they are dry, crisp and curling.
- Spread any flavoured butter (see page 72) and serve with soup.

FRENCH BREAD

PREPARATION TIME : 1 HR. 45 MINS.

COOKING TIME : 35 MINUTES   SERVES : 4 - 6
MAKES : 2 LOAVES

- 500 gms. white flour.
- 1$^1/_5$ cup (180 ml.) lukewarm water.
- 2 tsps. dried yeast.
- 1 tsp. sugar.
- 3 level tsps. salt mixed with 3 tsps. hot water for glazing.
- 1 vitamin C tablet crushed.
- 1 tsp. salt.

- Put lukewarm water in a small bowl. Sprinkle yeast and sugar. Leave for 15 minutes until frothy. Stir in the crushed vitamin C tablet.
- Sieve salt and flour in a bowl, add all the yeast liquid at once and mix to a soft and smooth dough.
- Place dough on a lightly floured board and knead until dough is firm and not sticky.
- Place the dough in a lightly oiled polythene bag and leave it to rise in a warm place for 25 minutes.
- Knead the dough again and divide into two parts. Roll each part into an oblong about 41 cm/16" role like a Swiss roll and place on a lightly floured baking tray. Make five diagonal slashes along the length of each loaf with a sharp knife.
- Brush the top of each loaf with salt water. Now leave the loaves in a warm place for 1 hour/to 1$^1/_2$ hours.
- Preheat the oven to 220°C - 425°F – gas mark 7. Place the baking tray on the upper-rack.
- Place a tin (use a small cake tin) of water under the rack. Bake for 15 minutes and remove the tin of water and bake for a further 20 minutes until very crisp and brown.
- It is best eaten on the same day.

BASIC VEGETABLE STOCK

PREPARATION TIME : 20 MINUTES	COOKING TIME : 4 HOURS MAKES : 9 CUPS

- 1½ kg. mixed vegetables (cabbage, carrots, turnips french beans, cauliflower).
- 2 large onions.
- 1 stick celery.
- 2 tbsps. barley, washed thoroughly.
- 2 tbsps. butter or margarine.
- 1 tsp. salt.
- 10 cups (2½ litres) hot water.

- Wash all vegetables and cut them roughly.
- Heat butter or margarine, fry vegetables for 5 minutes.
- Add barley, pour in water, bring to the boil, reduce heat, cover and simmer for 4 hours.
- Remove any scum, add salt and strain the liquid. Keeps fresh in refrigerator for 2-3 days.

BASIC BLANC DE VOLAILLE (CHICKEN STOCK OR WHITE STOCK)

PREPARATION TIME : 20 MINUTES	COOKING TIME : 1½ HOURS

- 1½ kg. boiled chicken.
- 1 large carrot washed, peeled and chopped.
- 4 black peppercorns.
- 1 onion stuck with 4 cloves.
- 1 stick celery chopped.
- 1 level tsp. salt.

- Remove flesh from the boiled chicken (You may use it for salad) and break the carcass into small pieces.
- Place bones in a pan with salt, pepper and water, bring to the boil slowly. Skim.
- Add remaining ingredients to the pan, cover tightly and simmer the stock for 1½ hours.
- Strain the stock and cool. Remove the fat when the stock is cold.
- Use as required. Store in refrigerator.

BASIC BONE STOCK

COOKING TIME : 5 HOURS

- 1 kg. lamb or mutton bones.
- 2 medium onions chopped.
- 1 large carrot.
- 1 medium turnip.
- 1 leek or 2 spring onions finely sliced.
- 5 black peppercorns.
- 1 level tsp. salt.
- ½ level tsp. meat extract or yeast extract.
- 10 cups water.

- Clean, wash, and remove excess fat from bones.
- Wash all vegetables. Place them in a large pan along with the bones, onions, salt, pepper and water. Bring to the boil. Reduce heat. Cover and simmer for 4 - 5 hours. Skim frequently.
- Strain the stock.
- Allow it to cool, then remove fat or lay strips of absorbent kitchen paper across the surface of the hot stock to remove excess fat.
- Store in refrigerator. Keeps fresh for 4 - 5 days. Use as required.

BASIC DASHI (JAPANESE STOCK)

COOKING TIME : 10 MINUTES

- 1½ litres water.
- 2" square dried Kalp (Kombu).
- 3 tbsps. dried flaked banitio (Katsuobushi).

- Bring water to the boil in a large sauce pan.
- Wash kalp well and add to the boiling water. Cook for 5 minutes.
- Add banitio. Bring to the boil again. Lower heat and remove immediately. Keep aside for 20 minutes, then strain and use as required.

Note: Readymade Dashi is also available in supari market or food stores.

BASIC

Quick Stocks

QUICK CHICKEN STOCK :
- Use chicken bouillon cubes mixed with water as directed. Use instead of chicken stock.

QUICK VEGETABLE STOCK :
- Use vegetable bouillon cubes instead of vegetable stock. Dissolve soup cubes with water as directed.

VEGETARIAN WHITE STOCK

PREPARATION TIME : 15 MINUTES	COOKING TIME : 1½ HRS.

- 2 cups chopped white pumpkin.
- 1 stick celery sliced.
- 1 onion chopped.
- 1 cup cauliflower.
- 1 turnip peeled and chopped.
- 2 cloves garlic crushed.
- 6 peppercorns.
- a few outer leaves of cabbage or lettuce chopped.
- 2 level tsps. salt.
- 1½ litres water.

- Boil water and salt in a large saucepan.
- Add all the ingredients, cover and lower heat. Simmer for 1½ hours over low heat.
- Rub through a sieve and strain. Can be stored in a refrigerator for 2 days.

BASIC

Miso
- A paste made from cooked, fermented soya beans, there are various types, white, red, beige and brownish each having varying degrees of salt. Japanese thick soups are mostly based on Miso, stirred into Dashi, the usual proportion being one tablespoon to one cup of stock.

Bean curd or toffu
- How to make (Refer book "The Flavours of China" page 38), made from soya milk, available in market, ready to use. Toffu is also sold in instant powdered form, easy to prepare and can be stored in refrigerator for 2-3 days.

Banitio (Katsuobushi)
- Dried Banitio is the favourite flavouring ingredient in Japanese cooking. Can be stored for a long time, or it can be bought and flaked. Dried banitio is extremely hard, one needs a special tool to break it.

Sake
- Japanese rice wine used also as an ingredient in soups, sauces and marinades. Brandy or dry sherry can be a good substitute.

Chilli Oil
- Break 20 dry chillies and fry in 1 cup oil until dark brown. Remove from heat, cool, strain and store.

Wine Vinegar
- Take a full bottle of red wine, remove the cork. Tie a muslin cloth over the mouth of the bottle and keep in the sun for a month. The wine will change into vinegar.

Coconut Milk
- 2 cups of grated coconut is mixed with 2 cups of hot water. Leave it to cool, then squeeze out the milk. If fresh coconut is not available, use packed flaked preserved coconut and squeeze out the milk. This is the thick coconut milk. Add hot water to the coconut residue and stir well. Allow to cool and then squeeze out the milk. This is the thin coconut milk.

Cottage Cheese or Panir
- 1 litre milk, $\frac{1}{2}$ cup yoghurt, 2 tbsps. lime juice. Heat the milk and bring it to a boil, stirring continuously to prevent cream forming on the top. Remove from heat, add lime juice and yoghurt. Stir till the milk curdles and let it stand for 20 minutes. Then strain through a muslin cloth and squeeze out all the liquid. The cream cheese thus formed is called 'Panir' or 'Chana'. For best result put a weight over the panir for half an hour.

Note: Instead of lime juice, tartaric acid can be used.

PIQUANT MAYONNAISE

PREPARATION TIME : 20 MINUTES | MAKES : 1½ CUPS

- 1 recipe classic mayonnaise (see page 84).
- 2 tbsps. tomato ketchup.
- 1 level tsp. chilli powder.
- 5 stuffed olives chopped (optional).

- Mix all ingredients with mayonnaise. Store in a cool place.

Vegetarian piquant mayonnaise:
Use 1 recipe of vegetarian mayonnaise instead of classic mayonnaise.

GREEN MAYONNAISE

- 1 recipe classic mayonnaise.
- 1 spring onion finely chopped.
- ½ cup finely chopped parsley or mint.
- 1 tbsp. finely chopped coriander.

- Mix all the ingredients together with mayonnaise. Store in a cool place.

Vegetarian green mayonnaise:
Use vegetarian mayonnaise instead of classic mayonnaise.

LEMON MAYONNAISE

- 1 recipe classic mayonnaise.
- 2 tbsps. lime or lemon juice.
- 1 tbsp. grated rind of lime or lemon.

- Mix all the ingredients together and store in a cool place until required.

VEGETARIAN LEMON MAYONNAISE

- 1 recipe eggless mayonnaise (see page 84).
- 2 tbsps. lime or lemon juice.
- 1 tbsp. grated lime or lemon rind.

- Mix all ingredients together.
- Cover and store in the refrigerator. Use within 2-3 days.

EGGLESS MAYONNAISE

PREPARATION TIME : 15 MINUTES

MAKES : 2 CUPS

- 1 small can evaporated milk.
- 1 cup (150 ml.) olive oil or groundnut oil.
- 4 tbsps. vinegar.
- 1 level tsp. salt.
- 1 level tsp. sugar.
- ½ level tsp. pepper.
- 1 level tsp. mustard powder.

- Place mustard, salt, pepper, sugar and evaporated milk in a bowl. Mix well.
- Using a hand beater, add olive oil drop by drop and keep beating thoroughly.
- Add vinegar and beat again until mixture is thickened. Store in a cool place.

CLASSIC MAYONNAISE

PREPARATION TIME : 15 MINUTES

MAKES : 1¼ CUPS

- 2 egg yolks (at room temperature).
- ³/₅ cup (90 ml.) olive oil.
- ½ level tsp. mustard powder.
- ¼ level tsp. pepper.
- 1 level tsp. sugar.
- 1 tsp. salt.
- 1 tbsp. lemon juice or vinegar.

- Put egg yolks with half the vinegar or lemon juice, mustard, salt, pepper and sugar. Mix well.
- Add oil drop by drop stirring all the time with a wooden spoon or a beater.
- Beat until sauce is thick and smooth.
- Gradually pour the rest of the oil in a steady stream, stirring constantly. The mayonnaise should be thick and have high gloss (if it becomes too thick, add a little more of the vinegar or lemon juice).
- When all the oil has been added, add remaining vinegar or lemon juice gradually and mix thoroughly. Store in a cool place.

MANGO MAYONNAISE

MAKES : 2 CUPS

- ⁴/₅ cup (120 ml.) classic mayonnaise (see page 84).
- 2 ripe mangoes.
- ¼ tsp. dry mustard.
- a few strands saffron.
- 1 tsp. vinegar.

- Peel and chop mangoes, put in a liquidizer, make a puree.
- Combine together in a large bowl mango puree, mustard, mayonnaise, saffron and vinegar. Mix well. Cover and store in refrigerator.

VEGETARIAN MANGO MAYONNAISE:

- Omit classic mayonnaise.
- Use ⁴/₅ cup (120 ml.) eggless mayonnaise and follow the recipe as given above.

ORANGE MAYONNAISE

PREPARATION TIME : 25 MINUTES

MAKES : 2 CUPS

- 1 recipe classic mayonnaise (see page 84).
- 3 tbsps. fresh orange juice.
- 2 tsps. grated orange rind.
- 3 orange segments, pith removed.

- Make mayonnaise as directed.
- Combine all the ingredients, except orange segments, together and beat well.
- Gently break the orange segments into small pieces and stir into the mayonnaise.
- Keep in the refrigerator until required.

Vegetarian Orange Mayonnaise:

- Replace classic mayonnaise with eggless mayonnaise.
- Follow the remaining recipe as given above.

CURRIED MAYONNAISE

| PREPARATION TIME : 10 MINUTES | NO COOKING | MAKES : 1½ CUPS |

- 1 recipe classic mayonnaise (see page 84)
- 2 level tsps. curry powder.
- 1 tbsp. lemon juice.
- ¼ tsp. garam masala.
- 1 tbsp. finely chopped green chillies.

- Combine all the ingredients in a bowl and mix well. Cover and store in the refrigerator. Keeps for 24 hours.

VEGETARIAN CURRIED MAYONNAISE

- 1 recipe eggless mayonnaise (see page 84).
- 2 level tsps. curry powder.
- ¼ tsp. garam masala.
- 1 tsp. chilli powder.
- 1 tbsp. lemon juice.
- 1 tbsp. finely chopped coriander.

- Put all the ingredients in a bowl and mix well. Store in a refrigerator. Keeps for 24 hours.

GARLIC VINEGAR

| | MAKES : 3¾ CUPS |

- 4 cups white vinegar.
- 8 cloves garlic crushed.

- Put garlic in a warm bowl.
- Heat vinegar in a sauce pan and bring to the boil. Remove from the heat and pour onto the garlic. Allow it to cool.
- Pour the liquid into a bottle with vinegar cover and leave in a cool place for 6 - 7 weeks until sufficiently flavoured. Strain through a muslin cloth.
- Rebottle again.

HOT MEXICAN DRESSING

PREPARATION TIME : 15 MINUTES

MAKES : 1¾ CUPS

- 4 large tomatoes blanched and chopped.
- 2 green chillies deseeded and chopped.
- 1 medium onion chopped.
- 1 level tsp. salt.
- 2 tbsps. olive oil.
- 1 tbsp. finely chopped parsley or mint.

- Press tomatoes through a sieve. Make a puree.
- Add all the ingredients and mix well. Keep in a cool place until required.

ITALIAN DRESSING

PREPARATION TIME : 5 MINUTES

MAKES : 1 CUP

- ³/₅ cup (90 ml.) olive oil.
- ¹/₅ cup (30 ml.) vinegar.
- 1 clove garlic crushed well.
- 1 level tsp. salt.
- ¼ level tsp. pepper.

- Place all ingredients in a bowl and beat well. Keep in a cool place until required.

ARABIAN SALAD DRESSING

PREPARATION TIME : 10 MINUTES	MAKES : 1 CUP

- ½ cup (75 ml.) olive oil.
- ½ cup (75 ml.) lime or lemon juice.
- 2 cloves garlic.
- 1 level tsp. salt.
- ½ level tsp. freshly ground pepper.

- Grind garlic and salt together and make a paste.
- Add remaining ingredients, beat thoroughly with a wooden spoon or a fork.

BASIC FRENCH DRESSING

PREPARATION TIME : 15 MINUTES	MAKES : 1½ CUPS

- 1½ cup oil or groundnut oil.
- ½ cup vinegar preferably wine vinegar (see page 82).
- 1 level tsp. salt.
- ½ level tsp. pepper.
- ½ level tsp. mustard powder.

- Put all the ingredients in a bowl and beat well. This sauce will separate when left to stand. Beat well again before using.

GARLIC FRENCH DRESSING :

PREPARATION TIME : 15 MINUTES	MAKES : 1½ CUPS

- 1 recipe basic French dressing (see page 88).
- 3 cloves garlic crushed a little.

- Add garlic before beating. Remove garlic before using or storing.

APPLE JUICE DRESSING

PREPARATION TIME : 5 MINUTES | NO COOKING | MAKES : 1¼ CUPS

- 1 cup apple juice.
- 4 tbsps. French dressing.
- 1 tsp. chilli powder.
- 1 tsp. roasted and ground cumin seeds.

- Mix all the ingredients together.

ORANGE DRESSING

PREPARATION TIME : 20 MINUTES | MAKES : 1½ CUPS

- 1 recipe basic French dressing (see page 88).
- 1 tsp. grated orange rind.
- 1 tsp. castor sugar.
- 2 tbsps. orange juice.
- ½ level tsp. chilli powder.

- Place all the ingredients in a bowl and beat well.
- If you want it more spicy, add 2 chopped green chillies to the dressing.

WHITE SALAD CREAM

PREPARATION TIME : 15 MINUTES | MAKES : 1¼ CUPS

- 1 cup (150 ml.) double cream.
- 2 egg whites beaten well.
- 3 tsps. lemon or lime juice.
- 1 level tsp. salt.
- ¼ level tsp. pepper.
- 1 tbsp. white vinegar.

- Beat the cream lightly, stir in vinegar, mix well.
- Add salt, pepper and lemon juice. Stir well and fold in beaten egg whites.

1000 ISLAND DRESSING

PREPARATION TIME : 30 MINUTES	MAKES : 3 CUPS

- 1 recipe classic mayonnaise (see page 84).
- 2 tbsps. tomato paste.
- 1 hard boiled egg chopped.
- 4 stuffed olive finely chopped.
- ½ tsp. tabasco sauce.
- 2 tsps. grated onion.
- 1½ cups basic French dressing.

- Put mayonnaise in a bowl and beat tomato paste, tabasco and onion into the mayonnaise.
- Add olives and egg, stir well.
- Gradually beat in the French dressing.

Vegetarian 1000 Island Dressing:
- Use eggless mayonnaise (see page 84) instead of classic mayonnaise.
- Omit egg. Use 2 tablespoons grated or crumbled plain Indian cottage cheese.
- Proceed as give above.

MUSTARD DRESSING

PREPARATION TIME : 5 MINUTES	NO COOKING	MAKES : 1 CUP

- 1 cup classic mayonnaise or fresh cream.
- 2 tbsps. mustard powder.
- 1 tsp. sugar.
- ½ tsp. salt.
- 1 tbsp. lime or lemon juice.
- 1 tbsp. grated onion.

- Put all the ingredients in a bowl and mix thoroughly.
- Excellent for beetroot salad or potato salad.